Paul Nash

Paul Nash

paintings and watercolours

Tate Gallery 1975

Exclusively distributed in France and Italy by Idea Books
46–8 rue de Montreuil, 75011 Paris and Via Cappuccio 21, 20123 Milan

ISBN 0 900874 95 3 paper 0 900874 96 1 cloth
Published by order of the Trustees 1975
for the exhibition of 12 November – 28 December 1975
Copyright © 1975 The Tate Gallery
Designed and published by the Tate Gallery Publications Department,
Millbank, London SW1P 4RG
Blocks by Augustan Engravers Ltd, London
Printed in Great Britain by Balding & Mansell Ltd, Wisbech, Cambs.

Contents

7 Foreword *Sir Norman Reid*

8 Plates

11 The Art of Paul Nash *Andrew Causey*

36 Paul Nash – a personal view *Margot Eates*

47 Catalogue

106 Chronology

111 Exhibitions

113 Bibliography

115 Lenders

Cover/jacket
Landscape of the Summer Solstice 1943
(detail of catalogue No.202)

Frontispiece
Paul Nash photographed by Helen Muspratt
of Ramsey & Muspratt, Oxford

Foreword

Although many of Paul Nash's paintings are well-known there has been no major exhibition of his work since 1948, the year of his memorial exhibition in this Gallery.

The present exhibition of paintings, watercolours and drawings is planned to give a full account of Nash's varied achievements in these media. Other aspects of his work, graphics and decorative arts are included in an exhibition at the Victoria and Albert Museum.

I should like here to thank the Paul Nash Trustee Selection Committee, Andrew Causey, Margot Eates and Anstice Shaw who have been unfailingly helpful at all stages. Andrew Causey has also written the introduction and catalogue entries and Margot Eates has provided a personal account of the artist. Through the generosity of the Nash Trustees Robin Langdon-Davies, Anstice Shaw and George Wingfield-Digby and the late Philip James we have been able to include a large number of colour plates in the catalogue.

We are as always indebted to all the lenders who have responded to our request for loans with enthusiasm. Some have lent very extensively from their collections and to these we are especially grateful and in particular to Lord Croft, the Edward James Foundation, the Imperial War Museum, the Victoria and Albert Museum and the National Gallery of Canada.

After the Tate showing the exhibition will be shown in four other places under the auspices of the Arts Council: Plymouth City Art Gallery; The Minories, Colchester; Cartwright Hall, Bradford; and Manchester City Art Gallery.

Norman Reid, Director

Plates

9 *The Three in the Night* 1913 (No.22)

10 *Ruined Country* 1917–18 (No.40)

    Sudden Storm 1918 (No.51)

19 *The Shore* 1923 (No.75)

    Landscape at Iden 1929 (No.113)

20 *Nest of the Siren* 1929–30 (No.118)

    Objects in Relation 1935 (No.153)

29 *Landscape from a Dream* 1936–8 (No.159)

    Landscape at Penn Pits 1937 (No.161)

30 *Pillar and Moon* 1932(?)–40 (No.181)

    Bomber in the Wood 1940 (No.184)

39 *November Moon* 1942 (No.196)

40 *The Sun Descending, study 7* 1945 (No.230)

    Eclipse of the Sunflower 1946(?) (No.233)

22 **The Three in the Night** 1913 (entry on p.54)

40 **Ruined Country** 1917–18 (entry on p.59)

51 **Sudden Storm** 1918 (entry on p.60)

The Art of Paul Nash

A substantial exhibition of Paul Nash's work shows that there is no simple category into which he can be fitted, and that access to his often complicated forms of expression is only slowly won. His artistic development was marked by bursts of creative activity, sometimes followed by brief periods when he seemed less sure of his direction. While the earliest pictures in the exhibition date from 1910, the full range of Nash's talent did not emerge until the late 1920s, and if none of his work after 1927 now remained, he would be known as a lyrical landscapist with a number of impressive works to his credit, but hardly as a figure of European stature. There are those who would like to see Nash limited to this role, and for them his exploration of continental modernism, Metaphysical art, Surrealism and Cubism, were fashionable flirtations through which he temporarily betrayed his real self.

The natural world afforded Nash unique spiritual refreshment, and he drew from nature in almost all periods of his career. The dramatic intensity of Nash's first landscapes in 1911–12, and the way they relate to his previous purely imaginative works, show that from the beginning Nash came to nature for more than its simple appearance. In the same way Nash's personal Surrealism was to a considerable extent a manifestation of his delight in nature, and the Surrealist events he constructed in landscapes are an outward realisation of the activities that had been hidden in the early landscape drawings and held covertly within the shadows of the woods and folded hills in the twenties. Surrealism helped to make Nash's feeling for the energy and vitality of nature actual. If Nash's later development seems occasionally unsure, it was not that in going beyond natural appearances he was trespassing on unauthorised territory, but that a native shyness and fear of losing his individuality made him reluctant to immerse himself as fully in Parisian modernism as he profitably might have.

Nash grew up within the tightly-structured framework of middle-class society; its public schooling, religious orthodoxy and conservative social attitudes were taken for granted in the family's protected world. He did not, however, have the full benefit of the secure family life assumed in the values of his class. His mother was chronically ill and increasingly away in nursing homes before her death in 1910 at the age of forty-nine. As a result much of Nash's childhood was spent with nannies and his school holidays with relatives in different parts of the country, so that he learned early to adjust to situations within the range of his upbringing; he was sociable, resourceful and popular, but to a considerable degree deprived of intimacy. His childhood experiences, as they are described in his autobiography, *Outline*,[1] show an uncommon imagination fabricating a private world more detached from everyday events than would have been likely if he had enjoyed a normal family life. As the eldest child of three, Paul assumed a special position in the family in the last years of his mother's life, becoming his father's confidant and helping to make the family's plans. His emotional immaturity and imaginative detachment were sometimes disguised by his often having to play an adult's role.

When Nash left school in 1906, he turned to illustration, which allowed his imagination to roam freely over a wide variety of literary themes, and he seems to have been writing poetry as keenly as he was drawing. In retrospect, illustration, as the most literary aspect of the visual arts, seems a natural starting point for an artist whose mature expression was to have a strong narrative content; but because it allowed him to project his imagination onto so much material that was read about but not seen and not necessarily deeply felt, it offered him little discipline compared with the rigorous and individual method of figure drawing he was taught at the Slade, which defeated him; optimistic at first, he quickly lost heart and continued to draw out of his head as much as from the model.[2]

As an artist-poet Nash was naturally drawn to Rossetti, and in 'Our Lady of Inspiration' Rossetti's influence is plain enough. The drawing more or less corresponds with a personal vision Nash described in *Outline*, which was mainly written in the 1930s: 'For now I needed an outlet for a new thing which had begun to stir in me and growing, gradually to absorb my whole mind and body, the strange torture of being in love. Henceforth, my world became inhabited by images of a face encircled with blue-black hair, with eyes wide-set and luminous, and a mouth, like an immature flower about to unfold. But the whole countenance, as I saw it so often in my dreams, seemed remote, untouched by human warmth, lit only by some other radiance which poured out of the eyes in their steady gaze – unaware of the mundane world; certainly unaware of me.'[3] It is natural to wonder what Nash in his adolescent state could have understood about ideal love, and he shared nothing of Rossetti's experience of the destructive power of passion; and indeed a little further on in *Outline* he admits that 'the face in the night sky had been only a dream'.[4]

Landscape offered Nash the possibility of a more personal artistic expression, and subjected him to greater discipline since he had to translate specific visual information into his drawings. But it was not for this that he explored landscape, as two letters to the playwright Gordon Bottomley show: 'I turned to landscape not for the landscape sake but for the "things behind"', and 'I hoped however you would find as much individualism & character in my landscape drawings for they are very real to me and I feel I succeed better in "finding myself" thro them than in any other direction'.[5] The forces he sought to expose related to himself and the landscapes were hardly less autobiographical than 'Our Lady of Inspiration'.

In the pictures of the garden of his home at Iver Heath, beginning with 'Bird Garden' of August 1911, Nash revealed a personal standpoint against nature. What is shown is in a sense familiar, and is there for everyone to see, but the presence of the unseen is inferred as well. The compositions are not too tightly closed: dramatic pools of light pick out individual features and shadows are cast across the pictures by things that are not themselves visible but offer the suggestion of activity beyond the edge of the paper.

Nash was gaining a confidence that made his drawing more forceful. Bottomley had advised him that 'the greatest mystery comes by the greatest definiteness', and Nash respected this advice.[6] Describing the garden in *Outline*, he wrote: 'It seemed to respond in a dramatic way to the influence of light. There were moments when, through this agency, the place took on a startling beauty, a beauty to my eyes wholly unreal. It was this "unreality", or rather this reality of another aspect of the accepted world, this mystery of clarity that was at once so elusive and so positive, that I now began to pursue.'[7] To realise this elusive experience, that was liable to fade back into common reality, Nash needed to be strong and searching in his drawing, to feel his way into the tree forms and build his layers of space through constant attention to nature.

Nash was especially drawn to a group of tall elms on one boundary of the garden; they were unique on account of their dominating presence and possessed a kind of permanence because they remained from an earlier pattern of nature. Standing over the newly planted garden of the home which had been built for the Nashes in 1901, they exercised an authority like that of ancestor figures over the new growth. In getting to know these survivors Nash made a link with the past: his home was in the county with which the Nashes had been associated as landowners and farmers since the sixteenth century. Nash's feeling for the special status of the trees emerges in one of his poems.

O dreaming trees sunk in a swoon of sleep
What have ye seen in those mysterious places?
What images? What faces?
What unknown pageant thro' these hollows moves
At night? What blood fights have ye seen?
What scenes of life & death? What haunted loves?[8]

The trees witness nocturnal struggles such as he had described more explicitly in the 1910 drawing 'Angel and Devil'. On finding that he could not approach these primal conflicts so literally and make them carry a convincing personal meaning, Nash turned to images of natural power and authority, like the elms, which he felt really related to him.

Wittenham Clumps, twin beechwoods capping a chalk outcrop near the Thames at Wallingford, was the only place to play a role as important as the garden in Nash's art before 1914. Nash described the Clumps as 'the Pyramids of my small world',[9] and several pictures of them have the feeling of a personal engagement. The distant views, 'The Wood on the Hill' and 'Wittenham Clumps', have a studied symmetry and effects of shading in the sky and over the landscape which help to establish the sense of their being special places, objectives in some drama but not easily approachable.

Nature was proving an excellent teacher, forcing Nash to test his imagination against visual reality and to relate his emotions to direct experience; its discipline released him from the risk of self-indulgence implicit in his earliest pictures. But his landscapes do relate to the imaginative works of 1910; they are dramatic and have Symbolist references, though these are not explicit and reflect private emotions.

Nash was still making drawings other than straight landscapes, and like those of 1910, they are night scenes in which the moon is generally the governing force. 'The Cliff to the North' was made on a holiday in Norfolk with his Slade friend Claughton Pellew-Harvey in December 1912:'At Mundsley', Nash wrote in *Outline*, 'I was chiefly impressed by the coast, the macabre fields of poppies on the yawning bluffs above the cold, bitter sea. The drawing I made showed the dark shadow of a figure approaching but not appearing in the picture. The shadow moved up the incline of the top of the cliff which was vividly cast into light and darkness by the moving beam from a lighthouse lower down the coast. In the semi-obscurity between, the wavering edge gave a glimpse of the cliff's crumbling face and the gnawing waves.'[10] Nash's tension at the time and his uncertainty about his personal direction emerges from his record of the kind of conversation he had with Pellew-Harvey: 'We talked about women mostly, I remember, where they came into the scheme of things, how they might share an artist's life', and, 'the question of marriage was most perplexing'.[11] Two months later Nash met his future wife, and in April they were engaged.

The description of the 'macabre fields of poppies' must have been a retrospective invention when Nash was writing *Outline* later; he could not have seen them in December and they do not appear in the picture. These emblems of sleep and death were inspired, perhaps, by Nash's memories of the war that was to come in 1914 and the poppy's special association with Flanders where he was to serve. The force of the imagery in the drawing, the edge of the cliff like a zig-zag tear and the shadow thrown across the opposite diagonal, suggests a new maturity, which perhaps extended to an understanding of the fateful triangle of woman, love and death, and an insight into the mainsprings of Rossetti's art now that he was past the need to imitate his style.

Nash described a second imaginative drawing, 'The Pyramids in the Sea', to Bottomley as 'a queer drawing of pyramids crashing about in the sea in an uncanny eclipsed moonlight',[12] which again echoes Nash's sense of the hostility of the sea at night, since the pyramids do not appear markedly unstable. Their firm structured shapes contrast with the undulating waves, establishing a broad antithesis between chaos and form. The picture's simple design is direct and strong, easily engaging and holding the spectator's attention, yet it refers to issues that are deeply personal. The pyramids relate to the different kinds of solid object that Nash used in the late 1920s as object-personages, equivalents for the human form, and it is perhaps no coincidence that 'Lavengro and Isopel in the Dingle', one of the few survivors from among the many figure subjects Nash was doing in 1912–13, is composed of a series of linked triangles: Lavengro makes one, his legs alone another, Isopel a third, and the whole composition, figures and trees together, makes a fourth, subsuming all the lesser ones.

Nash came to artistic maturity at an awkward time. While acknowledging that nineteenth-century images were no longer directly relevant, he needed some equivalent for the intense expression of Rossetti and the fin-de-siècle. The literary-poetic movement that flourished on the reaction against the fin-de-siècle, found its verbal expression in Georgian poetry and an artistic manifestation in the romany pictures of Augustus John, appealed to Nash. His reading tended towards novelists and poets whose work had a strong landscape content; he especially admired the 'tramp' poet, W. H. Davies, who later bought two of his pictures, and his choice of George Borrow's *Lavengro* as a subject for illustration exemplifies his sense of himself as a wanderer in nature.

The passion that inspired 'The Pyramids in the Sea' and 'The Cliff to the North' could not for long be satisfied with Georgianism. When Roger Fry welcomed Nash to Bloomsbury in 1914 and encouraged him to take a substantial role in the activities of the first artistic avant-garde that England had had in the twentieth century, Nash still did not seem to have found the stimulus he needed. This was due to some extent to the war and to clashes of personality which excluded Nash from Bloomsbury after 1918, but fundamentally Bloomsbury painting did not have the dynamic charge to satisfy Nash. Among contemporaries only Wyndham Lewis painted with the urgency Nash could learn from, but, having so little artistic education, Nash had no access before the war to Lewis's painting with its complex understanding of Cubism, Matisse and primitive art.

Nash's progress between 1910 and 1912 was striking, but nevertheless limited by a lack of technical advance. In 1912 he was still entirely dependent on draughtsmanship. His 1910 pictures related to wood engraving, and some of his subsequent landscapes to etching, which is not surprising considering his early interest in illustration, and which – more than his passion for night scenes – explains why he was so slow in coming to a mature use of colour. The urgent flow of his ideas seems to have left him little time to develop his method, so that a great deal of groundwork had still to be covered after the war.

But despite their technical limitations the early drawings are convincing works, full of excitement, and are authentic accounts of a sensitive personality feeling for a relationship with the rest of the natural world, exteriorising energy that is uncertainly felt but is made into something constructive by the process of realisation. Nash needed tremendous tenacity in his search because he had so little experience of discipline and had to find out so much for himself. But the experience of discovery was itself enthralling. He wrote to Bottomley in 1945: 'When I came to look into the early drawings I lived again that wonderful hour. I could feel myself making those drawings – in some ways the best I ever did to this day.'[13]

Nash's first war pictures reflect the relative lack of activity in the part of the Ypres Salient where he served between March and May 1917. 'Chaos Decoratif', with its arrangement of ladders and duckboards against dense foliage with little distance showing, recalls prewar landscapes like the 1914 'Orchard'. 'Old Front Line. St. Eloi' is more obviously a war landscape, but has the melancholy air of a deserted place far from the actual activity of war.

When Nash returned to the front as an official artist in November in the wake of Passchendaele, he found a quite different scene. His letters home in the spring record the enigmatic unreality of the trench landscapes with flowers blooming on the trench parapets and burgeoning plant life everywhere making good man's damage to the landscape; but the summer and autumn fighting, and almost continuous rain since August, converted the clay-bedded Flanders plain into a turmoil of mud and water. He did not find it easy in his pictures to approach the war through the makers of war. It was not that he was inhumane or resigned to human suffering: 'Out there men have been thinking, living so near to silence and death, their thoughts have been furious, keen and living has been alive', he wrote to his wife.[14] But he found better personal access to the tragedy in the scars left on the landscape. He was observant of the moods of nature and could realise his own passion through them. The cruelty of human actions seemed more truthfully recorded in the landscape, or at least more available to him as an artist, since nothing he could do with the individual human figure could make it express the gravity of the situation.

A new objectivity was necessary in his drawings of Passchendaele to help carry the emotional burden of horror Nash experienced. His landscapes were more directly represented, not conventionally realist but the product of an immediate reaction. Nash was helped in this by C. R. W. Nevinson, the English artist most experienced in the recording of war, whose work Nash would have known from exhibitions back to 1915. Nash used Nevinson's greater knowledge of the modern styles, the angular forms of Cubism and Vorticism, to sharpen his presentation.

Nash's exhibition of war paintings in 1918 included his first surviving oils, which are considerable achievements considering that he had no training in the medium and was painting under the pressure of time. The most impressive is 'We are Making a New World' which, with its hard paint surface and economical use of bold frontal shapes, is simpler but more daring than any of the other oils of the war. Though developed from a battlefield drawing, 'Sunrise. Inverness Copse', it is a Symbolist painting. The pale sun, organ of future regeneration, can be thought of as spreading its rays through the sky of blood which it will dispel or draw into itself. On the other hand Nash's sphere, both in the drawing and the oil painting, illuminates the landscape with a pale, whitish light and, if it were not for the title of the drawing, would be naturally taken for the moon. Nash may have been maintaining a deliberate ambiguity: the sphere is either the regenerating sun or it is the sacrificial moon about to suffuse itself with the blood of the soldiers who were victims of a situation not of their making and outside their understanding.

Although 'We are Making a New World' is a Symbolist painting, it is free of what Nash would have regarded as the cumbersome appurtenances of traditional Symbolist art. Ideas that previously had been signalled by iconographical detail, Nash brought out through colour and by means of the symmetries and stylisations which announce that this is no longer *a* but *the* Flanders landscape. This was another step in the direction Nash had been taking in 1911–12: he had found then that ideas he had been presenting figuratively could be more meaningful in landscape form, and that the quite simple contrasts of shape which he found to have natural authority in 'The Pyramids in the Sea' could be equally valid when found, as in 'We are Making a New World', in natural forms.

Nash was unlucky that his war pictures brought him to the forefront of English painting just as artists were turning their back on the prewar mood of experiment. There were no exhibitions of major contemporary continental artists in London after the mixed show organised by the Sitwell brothers at Heal's in August 1919 and the Matisse and Picasso shows at the Leicester Galleries (1919 and 1921), until the de Chirico exhibition at Tooth's in 1928. Nor was there any art periodical fulfilling the role of *The Criterion* (from 1922) in literature of making advanced ideas from continental countries available to an English audience. And for Nash, unlike Lewis, there was no alternative way forward through writing. Nash was living out of London in the twenties, unable to afford much travel and virtually out of contact with other artists.

The failure of an avant-garde to emerge after the war had serious implications for Nash. It did not prevent his art from progressing; the development away from the harsh, nervous draughtsmanship of the wartime 'The Cherry Orchard', through the looser and more animated 'Windy Hill' to the unprecedentedly relaxed 'Towards Stone' measures Nash's immense progress in watercolour between 1917 and 1921. But it did circumscribe his possible range of development because nothing more recent than Post-Impressionism and the early stages of Cubism was available for English painters to assimilate. Considering the situation, Nash's achievement in the twenties seems impressive.

Of the places where Nash worked in the ten years after the war only Dymchurch on the Kent coast, with its vast length of wall built to protect Romney Marsh from flooding by the sea, touched Nash's imagination to the degree Iver Heath and Wittenham had before the war. From the simple but remarkable appearance of the place Nash evolved a complex mythology related to ideas of vulnerability, attack, pursuit and defence, and having personal references to himself as well as to the external scene. Nash found copious material for his work at Dymchurch until 1925, when it suddenly lost its magic and the Nashes moved to Iden, an inland village in Sussex, and Nash announced decisively to Anthony Bertram: 'I shall never work there any more', and reflected: 'A place like that and its effect on me – one's effect on it. It's a curious record formally and psychologically when you see the whole set of designs together.'[15] This sense that Nash rejected Dymchurch, rather than simply left it to live somewhere else, is a symptom of the intensely personal and very demanding relationship he formed with places. When they were no longer relevant to his mood he moved on.

The tenor of the Dymchurch pictures, the pattern of the waves breaking against the shore and the wall, the sense of the wall as a bastion or defence, and the hooded figure in 'The Steps' and 'Night Tide', a throwback to 'The Cliff to the North', all seem to infer threat and insecurity. The drama was personal; Nash's early experience of the sea had been 'cold and cruel',[16] and now he found himself in a situation that corresponded to poetic images that, with his interest in Romantic poetry, he knew and was attracted to: the sea as materialism in Blake and Coleridge, and as a symbol of the power of woman and man's willingness to die in many Victorian poets. The endlessness of the sea's repeated movements corresponds with the apparent infinity of time that Shelley cursed in 'Time':

Unfathomable sea! Whose waves are years
Oceans of Time, whose waters of deep woe
Are brackish with the salt of human tears.

The degree to which Nash realised his emotions at Dymchurch in terms of place is unusual even for him, and throws into relief his tense state which culminated in a nervous collapse in 1921. Nash was uncertain about the direction of his art, he suffered the rancour of artists who were jealous of his success as a war artist, and he had become alienated from Bloomsbury artists. But the context of the Dymchurch pictures and Nash's unsettled state of mind was still the war: Nash was haunted by the lonely soldiers in the great waste, and his two tiny figures in 'Sea Wall', whom R. H. Wilenski described sympathetically as 'fantastic figures who flutter on the asphalt like dry leaves at the mercy of the elements',[17] are like reincarnations in a world that is still barren.

By the middle of the twenties Nash had brought his oil painting to a standard only hinted at in the early postwar paintings. 'Chestnut Waters', with its voluptuous swathes of foliage, was the centrepiece of his 1924 exhibition at the Leicester Galleries and a picture Nash was particularly proud of. Oils like 'Pond in the Fields' and 'Savernake' possess a distinct authority on account of their carefully balanced symmetries. But even when they were made it must have been evident that they were the culmination of a development which, if further refined, would become a constriction.

75 **The Shore** 1923 (entry on p.64)

113 **Landscape at Iden** 1929 (entry on p.75)

118 **Nest of the Siren**
1929–30 (entry on p.76)

153 **Objects in Relation** 1935 (entry on p.86)

Nash's dilemma was well expressed by *The Times* art critic, Charles Marriott, who wrote in his review of the 1928 London Group exhibition that English painters 'have steadily and not too rapidly advanced towards more and more organised design, or towards the exact expression of their sensibility'. He said of Nash that 'he has worked on his manner and improved it out of all knowledge . . . . But as a designer Mr Nash has remained the same. For it is not along this line that he has worked'.[18] In a letter to his wife Nash endorsed Marriott's criticism: 'He emphasises the strength which is the weakness of the modern English mind, underlining our national label, Safety First . . . . The French appeal more to me. They have reached out, they have real mental daring. "Tactic audacity" says Cocteau "is knowing how to go too far." Marriot[t] is right I feel when he says that as a designer I have remained stationary.'[19]

Nash's determination to climb out of the rut resulted in 1928–30 in the most distinctive changes his painting ever underwent. He had sensed his predicament earlier, but had been only vaguely aware of potential solutions. The Dymchurch wall had already suggested the possibility of abstraction because of its shape. In 'The Shore', in which he was least concerned with Symbolism, Nash reduced his formal elements to a minimum which gave a new independence to the sharp, clear colours. In an interview in 1926 Nash was reported as being interested in 'what Cocteau calls the liberation of geometry',[20] and his only surviving completely abstract work of the twenties, the first drawing for 'Opening', dates from 1927. The range of Nash's experiment may have been wider, because Anthony Bertram recorded in 1927 that Nash was 'testing the possibilities of abstract design as an alternative method of expressing the order which he otherwise seeks to impose upon representation'.[21] This notion of a formal order imposed upon visual reality was a more available basis for development for an English painter in the mid-twenties than was pure abstraction. Still life, which attracted Nash very little until he turned his attention to it seriously in 1926–7, suited his requirements as he began to explore more structural solutions. It was in this area that Nash worked out a tighter more methodical application of paint which was to become the hallmark of a new painting style in 1929.

A consequence of Nash's determination to expand the range of his art was a reconsideration of material he already had in hand. Landscapes he had developed from his continental trip of 1924–5 had not been very successful, but now, in 'The Tower', 'Blue House on the Shore' and 'Souvenir of Florence', he used forms, substantial closed objects with an uncompromising but mysterious presence, which are quite different from any of the other subjects he had discovered on the trip and had already worked up into oil paintings, though they do recall the 1924 painting 'Dymchurch Steps'. These solid forms, palpable presences, unmistakably there yet retaining their meaning within themselves, are precursors of Nash's object-personages. They are not simply a means of avoiding straightforward figuration, they describe Nash's feeling for the fusion of the forthright and the inscrutable which characterises the human presence.

The figure had been a recurrent problem for Nash since he had been at the Slade. In 1927 he had told his friend Percy Withers that 'my next step is a study of the human figure for which I am very ill-equipped at present';[22] he included oil studies of the head and nude in his 1928 show, but had not liked them when they were hung, and had withdrawn and destroyed them. Nash found it difficult to transcend the commonplace in the representation of the figure. In some of his war pictures he had tried to expose the emotional intensity of life in the shadow of death, and at Dymchurch he had shown the tenuousness of existence through the tiny figures on the wall. Margaret Nash recorded[23] that when they were in Italy in 1925 Paul was particularly drawn to the frescoes in the Campo Santo at Pisa. The explosive expressions on the faces of the figures in the frescoes there by the fifteenth-century Maestro del Trionfo della Morte would have been an obvious stimulus to an artist searching for ways to convey his sense of the vulnerability of existence and the constant imminence of death. They could be of no direct use to Nash because for him, as for most serious painters of his generation, the figurative tradition was too effete to record such turbulence. Though Nash made no attempts to paint the figure after 1928, he had not abandoned his search: a feeling for the strength of passions and the frailty of life underlies the calm symmetries of his semi-abstract compositions in 1928–9.

Nash's success in recapturing the dramatic quality which he had not been able to sustain in his painting since Dymchurch was partly inspired by the art of Giorgio de Chirico, which was shown in London in 1928. De Chirico's paintings, especially those based on the Renaissance architecture of Italian cities which he made in Paris between 1912 and 1914, were imbued with intensity of feeling by means that included unusual architectural designs, exaggerated perspectives and emotive contrasts between foreground and distance. Nash, in his 1929 'Landscape at Iden', introduced more firmly structured individual elements than he was accustomed to, distortions of perspective to enhance the element of surprise in objects that were not remarkable in themselves, and he used the informality of the distant hills to release the tension built up by the circumscribed space of the foreground. The protagonists in Nash's drama are a stake in the foreground and a log basket nearby which recall the rake and basket that accompany the two figures in Jean-François Millet's 'The Angelus'. Nash's choice of emblematic representation of the figures in preference to figuration echoes his presentation in 'We are Making a New World', and is in line with his recent research into inanimate objects that would help to define human dramas.

In the mid-twenties Nash had been implicitly denying the Symbolist basis of his art, but finding in de Chirico a contemporary of substantial reputation able to develop Symbolist themes semi-figuratively, Nash was encouraged to renew his own search in that direction. 'Landscape at Iden' is full of detail and inference realised in such a way that the images are never compromised by imprecision and the spectator is brought without fuss within the picture's terms of reference. Dry and ordered application of paint complements the clarity of the intellectual organisation, and at the same time recovers what Nash had wanted from the first, 'this reality of another aspect of the accepted world, this mystery of clarity that was at once so elusive and so positive'.

In February 1929 Nash's father died. Margaret Nash told Bertram that 'nothing in their whole married life so profoundly affected her husband as his father's death',[24] and Nash's letters bear this out. He wrote to a friend, Hilda Felce: 'It was a tragic business losing my Dad. As you know I loved him very much . . . . A part of my life goes with him for in so many ways he and I were linked.'[25]

Nash had been close to his father since the prolonged illness and early death of his mother, which had marked his early life and left him with a sense of the closeness of death that the war had augmented. Nash's slow recovery from the disorientation of the war had been interrupted by the serious nervous collapse in 1921, itself triggered off by the discovery of his father unconscious and the momentary belief that he was dead. The outward calm of Nash's life in the mid-twenties belies the fact that the horror of the war was ineradicably fixed in his memory. Nash had a powerful sense of family; his preoccupation in 1911–12 with the landscape at Iver Heath was like an assumption of responsibility in the family, since the land was historically close to Nash territory, and the sale of the family home coming on top of the death of his father gave him an added sense of loss.[26]

'February', titled after the month of his father's death, shows a stump with chopper stuck into it in the extreme foreground, so that the event it symbolises seems very close to the artist himself, as if he were even assuming some responsibility. The manner in which Nash's health at different times appears connected with his father's recalls his remark that 'in so many ways he and I were linked', and this, together with his feeling for family ties, suggests an affinity with the anthropological archetype of the hieratic succession to leadership, the act of assumption of power which commits the holder to eventual death as Nash was to find it described in Frazer's *The Golden Bough*, a major source of ideas for his last paintings when he was coming to terms with his own imminent death. In 1930 Nash suffered the first onset of the asthma which Lord Horder, the physician he consulted in 1945, is reported to have diagnosed as 'resulting in a person of unusually hypersensitive tension',[27] and which was to cause his death from heart failure in 1946.

In other paintings of 1929 Nash approached the subject of his father's death with more reserve. In 'Month of March', for instance, which follows 'February' in the sequence of titles, Nash turned to a subject which shows his own home and garden at Iden carried out in his most advanced style. The contrast suggests that Nash may have been concerned lest the openness of the symbolism in 'February' would lead to weakness. Nevertheless the liberation implicit in 'February' between the foreground crisis and the freedom of the distant birds hovering over the gate is echoed by the sequence in the 'Month of March' of the open casement, the tripodal ladder and the clouds.

In February 1930 the Nashes left for a holiday in the South of France with the painter Edward Burra and their friend Ruth Clark. Margaret Nash recorded that 'Edward Burra wanted to visit Toulon and stay at the hotel which he had visited the previous summer with Jean Cocteau and his strange menagerie of friends. Accordingly we found ourselves in the Hôtel du Port which overlooked the harbour at Toulon, and in the distance, on the other side of the harbour, lay the French fleet'. She went on to recall the origins of the painting 'Harbour and Room' which shows 'a French man o' war sailing into our bedroom; the idea resulting from the reflection of one of the ships in the very large mirror which hung in front of our bed'.[28] The illusion that the water was actually in the room must surely have called to Nash's mind the sea threatening the wall at Dymchurch, and maybe even the waves gnawing at the coast in 'The Cliff to the North'. A link between Nash's work now and his early Symbolist art was inferred by the painter John Armstrong, whose interests both in Surrealist imagery and dramatic presentation were close to Nash's, when he wrote in 1932 of the way 'the waves that threatened the pyramids twenty years ago are sweeping onwards'.[29] His reference to 'The Pyramids in the Sea' points to the origin in Nash's art of this theme of the structured or closed object – the pyramid, the sea wall or the room – jeopardised by the destructive incursion of the sea.

The two important paintings to result from the Toulon stay, 'Harbour and Room' and 'Voyages of the Moon', share the central significance of the mirrored image. Margaret Nash's recollection that Toulon was Burra's choice because he had been there previously with Cocteau seems especially relevant since Cocteau used the mirror in *Orphée* as the symbol of the threshold between life and death. 'I shall tell you the secret of secrets', Cocteau said. 'Mirrors are the doors by which Death comes and goes.'[30] Margaret Nash recalled that Paul at this time was 'very interested in the release of the dream',[31] and now, as in 1911–12, there is a high proportion of night scenes in his work. If Nash envisaged the harbour scene as a metaphor for death, it was not an absolute death, but a strengthening resignation to sleep and the unconscious, an allegory of the legendary night sea voyage in search of consciousness.

Nash's imaginative grasp of the possibilities offered by unusual visual illusions was not something completely new so much as an extension of his ability to make places he related to personally, such as Iver Heath and Dymchurch, surrender their commonplace existence in exchange for a new and heightened reality. But Surrealism introduced a new flexibility and, in particular, broke down traditional categories of subject matter. As he developed the theme of the room interior, from 'Interior' through 'Coronilla' to 'Harbour and Room' and 'Nest of the Siren', Nash was able to introduce ideas which his earlier pictures could not have carried.

Just as in 1928–9 Nash had seen ways of using material gathered as early as 1924–5, so in 1930 he was able to complete 'Nest of the Siren' for which the original impulse had been his discovery of a wooden siren figure from a boat decorating a huxter's cart in Caen in June 1928. The painting had been begun in 1929, but perhaps only after the Toulon trip was Nash able to formulate the complex sensations – excitement, risk, threat and pleasure – that the subject seems to have suggested. 'Nest of the Siren' is a painting of flamboyant presence, powerful imagery and, for Nash, unusually strong colouring; but it is reserved in what it actually gives away. Though constructed from elements of visual reality, it is not at all naturalistic: not only is the siren dissociated from the cart and given a new command over her environment, but despite the cobblestones which suggest a street, the panelling indicates an interior, the siren's lair. For Nash, siren and muse are inseparable complements, and it is no more true that the siren here is purposelessly evil or without a constructive role than that 'Harbour and Room' is a wholly threatening and pessimistic picture.

Nash was emboldened in his new paintings by his discovery that elements in contemporary French culture endorsed themes in his own painting. From the time he first saw a large collection of modern French painting, at Léonce Rosenberg's gallery in February 1929,[32] he followed French developments keenly, but he never made personal friendships with French artists or visited their studios. It was not that he lacked commitment to continental modernism in so far as it could enrich his art, but at the age of forty and unable to speak the language, he found direct involvement in the Parisian art world outside his range.

Nash's most productive friendship at this time was with the American poet and novelist Conrad Aiken, a near neighbour at Rye who became a close friend around 1930. Their sensibilities were remarkably similar. Thus Aiken's lines: 'We must think/that all we know is lost, or only dream/That dreams are real, and real things only dream'[33] would have been especially meaningful to Nash just after the Toulon visit; and Aiken's poem 'Cliff Meeting', which he recorded in his autobiography *Ushant* was the result of personal failure in love and had given him a 'new concept of the terrible – almost evil – power of love, its power for destruction and horror',[34] would have struck a chord in Nash thinking back to 'The Cliff to the North'. It is less a question of individual instances of Aiken's influence than of Aiken validating early work whose status Nash himself had long been uncertain of. Nash must have been excited to find the personally revealing imagery of his most imaginative work endorsed by the experience of another artist. In 1926 Nash had shied off discussion of his 1922 Dymchurch drawing 'Night Tide' because he thought it too romantic;[35] but in July 1931 he bought it back from the Coke sale at Sotheby's. His 1931 retrospective at Oxford included 'A Lane in Blue', probably the first prewar drawing to be shown in an exhibition since 1914.

'Nest of the Siren' was not only a major subject painting but also an attempt by Nash to be dramatic without using very deep space. After the Toulon visit there is a clear shift in his interest away from the kind of deep space he had found in de Chirico to a concern with surface pattern and texture which emerged in more abstract paintings. In 1937 Nash was to write that 'a few attempts to escape into the refuge of abstract design proved me unsuited',[36] but if it is to the abstract and semi-abstract work of 1930–31 that he was referring, his self-criticism seems exaggerated.[37] 'Kinetic Feature', which is probably the only wholly non-figurative oil painting by Nash now surviving, is indeed an unarresting painting, its deficiencies revealing themselves by contrast with the comparable 'Lares' and 'Opening', in which crisp and precise kinds of paint application, dotting and stippling, enrich the surface. They are not properly abstract paintings – the first was based on the design of a fireplace and the second shows a stone arch opening onto a view of the sea – but their handling in terms of the interlocking planes of decorative late Cubism is completely convincing. In two exhibition reviews he wrote in 1931, of London exhibitions of Picasso and the primitive André Bauchant, Nash stressed the character of the actual paint surface as an attribute of quality in these artists' works,[38] and it was obviously something he was considering at the time in his own painting. This was Nash's most successful adaptation of Cubism. It is a pity he did not pursue it further, and proves how deeply engrained a feeling for dramatic space was in his aesthetic.

By 1931 the immense impetus Nash had felt since 1928 was levelling off, and his direction was becoming less clear. His progress was also controlled by external events. His income from sales of pictures fell disastrously in 1931 because of the economic situation,[39] writing and illustrating took up much of his time,[40] and, possibly because his oils were not selling, he switched primarily to watercolour which he had all but abandoned between 1926 and 1930. Early in 1933 Nash was seriously ill with bronchitis and did very little work for the whole year. In July, however, while recuperating at Marlborough, he had his first sight of the Avebury megaliths, and began to evolve a new interest in the distant past and its manifestations in landscape, which lasted in different ways until 1938. The memory of Avebury overshadowed his work the next winter which, for the sake of his health, he spent in the South of France. Neither Paris nor the Riviera seemed to stimulate him or engender new subjects as in 1930. Nash was no longer absorbed by the postulates of 'Harbour and Room' which, now that he was thinking of Avebury, seemed perhaps too intellectual and lacking in sensuousness for his aesthetic which, since 1911, had developed chiefly as a series of responses to nature. 'The hard cold stone, the rasping grass, the intricate architecture of trees and waves or the brittle sculpture of a dead leaf – I cannot translate altogether beyond their own image, without suffering in spirit', Nash wrote in 1935.[41] Avebury was the turning point which was confirmed the following summer when he discovered on Romney Marsh the two pieces of driftwood which became his first 'found object', 'Marsh Personage'. He then started to collect natural objects which he felt had status and personality – flints and other stones, bones, and jetsam from the sea – and they became protagonists in new dramas.

Nash was unsure at first of his new direction, but too confident in his ability to invest so-called inanimate things with vitality to revert to simple landscape painting. He wrote to Bertram in April 1934: 'I am beginning now to find my way between the claims of "Abstractions" and pure interpretation. As you know, I am far too interested in the character of landscape and natural forms generally . . . ever to abandon painting *after* nature of some kind or other. But I want a wider aspect, a different angle of vision as it were. This I am beginning to find through symbolism and in the power of association – not the rather freakish unlikely association of objects, so much as the *right* association as I feel it to be. It is only another step in the mystery of relationship. We are accustomed to seek forms which inter-relate, colours which are significant by juxtaposition. I desire to penetrate further . . . to include a relation of spiritual personality.'[42]

In such paintings as 'Equivalents for the Megaliths' and 'Objects in Relation' Nash found this relationship by rigorous abstraction from visual reality, careful spacing, a degree of symmetry, by colour which, though not naturalistic, refers back to the original subject, and above all by firm orderly brushwork which activates the surface, affirms the palpability of the forms, and establishes the objects as personages that respond directly to the spectator's enquiry. Nash still faced the predicament he had had with his abstract paintings in 1930–31. Where he was able, as in these 1935 pictures and in 'Opening' and 'Lares' among the earlier ones, to vitalise the actual paint surface convincingly, the forms always come alive, whether – as in 1931 – they are composed in shallow space, or, in 1935, in deep space. But when he painted, as he did his first Avebury oil painting, 'Landscape of the Megaliths', with an even, relatively untextured surface, as he had the earlier 'Kinetic Feature', the painting remained lifeless, the weak naturalism of the colour and the vestigial landscape references working against the degree of abstraction that the artist intended.

Nash never painted the megaliths naturalistically, but tested different ways of manifesting the sense of power and animation he felt them to have; his sense of their rugged, almost animal character is expressed in 'Stone Tree' in which the coarse contour of the massive stone presses towards the edge of the canvas. Nash was interested in the polarity between rough-hewn forms and the perfected geometrical shapes of 'Equivalents for the Megaliths' and 'Objects in Relation', where he represented the stones in terms of contemporary sculptural and machine-made forms which have minimal reference to their actual shape; and in 'Event on the Downs' he posed the rough against the smooth, the tree stump against the tennis ball. Primitive energy and the process of its differentiation were an enduring preoccupation in his art, most of all in the thirties, and in formal terms Nash perhaps saw the beginning and end of the process represented in this contrast.

Nash's feeling for the past, stimulated by Avebury, expanded when he was living at Swanage in 1934–6 and exploring the countryside gathering material for his *Dorset Shell Guide*.[43] His interest in the archaic realised through landscape was further provoked by Max Ernst, whose painting Nash had been interested in since it was shown at the Mayor Gallery in 1933.[44] Ernst's influence was never directly stylistic as de Chirico's had been, but was more a matter of a shared feeling for certain kinds of subject; Ernst's primeval ruined and overgrown cities may have struck a chord in Nash's mind with Avebury which appealed to Nash because it had not then been reinstated and many of the stones were in what he called their 'wild state',[45] half-buried in undergrowth; but above all it was Ernst's series of the forest, seat of irrational and instinctive forces, that Nash admired.[46]

The richness of Ernst's ideas did not fully emerge into Nash's art till the important series of watercolours he showed at the Redfern Gallery in 1937. 'Wood of the Nightmares' Tales' is a startling evocation of a primordial world with great horse-tails, which grew in carboniferous swamps some two hundred million years ago, metamorphosed into a nightmare forest. Nash was not concerned with the past for its own sake, but as a source of images of the world in a more primitive state which, in view especially of the unusually plain phallic connotations of the trees in 'Wood of the Nightmares' Tales', could be regarded as analogues for the irrational instincts that undermine human control. 'The Landscape at Penn Pits' is less obviously evocatory of the past, but the arrangement of the picture suggests that natural features are being used as archetypes. The sun shining through the tree trunks across the curving banks of earth recalls 'We are Making a New World', but here there is a feeling of a burgeoning vitality. In using 'The Landscape at Penn Pits' together with 'The Pyramids in the Sea' – two pictures in which firm, upright elements emerge from more sensuous feminine forms – to illustrate an excerpt from his autobiography published in 1938,[47] Nash made a revealing comparison.

The International Surrealist Exhibition in London in June 1936 made Nash once more consider his position against continental modernism. The oil version of 'Harbour and Room' was first shown here and, against the megalith pictures it hung with, must have shown how far Nash had moved outside the ambience of Parisian painting since 1930. In the period between the summer of 1936 and May 1938, when he had his first major exhibition of oil paintings for ten years, at the Leicester Galleries, he again looked carefully at Surrealism, especially the work of Magritte, and achieved a number of major pictures, the most striking of which is 'Landscape from a Dream', with its strong and luminous colouring that looks forward to the brilliance of 'Landscape of the Vernal Equinox' and the oil landscapes of 1943–5.

After 1938 Nash found less need for the elaborate kind of symbolism displayed in 'Landscape from a Dream'; he was gradually becoming more self-sufficient and able to encapsulate emotion within the structure of natural and

159 **Landscape from a Dream** 1936–8 (entry on p.87)

161 **Landscape at Penn Pits** 1937 (entry on p.87)

181 **Pillar and Moon** 1932(?)–40 (entry on p.92)

184 **Bomber in the Wood** 1940 (entry on p.94)

observed forms, as he did simply and authoritatively in 'Pillar and Moon'. He may also have been deterred by the way the 1936 exhibition initiated a Surrealist vogue in England, permitting less-experienced artists to take easy possession of ground he had gradually made his own, infringing the privacy of symbols that for him were deeply felt, and degrading them into a language of signs.

The painting of de Chirico and the Surrealists had served Nash well, though the affinities between his early work and his post-1928 pictures confirms the claim he made to Herbert Read in 1942 that 'I did not find Surrealism, Surrealism found me';[48] undoubtedly Nash's readiness for Surrealism contributed to the immediate success with which he was able to develop it constructively and according to a rational plan. Surrealism tested his imagination in many ways, broadened the range of his subject matter, extended and refined his symbolism, revealed to him new ways of expressing his sense of fear, primitiveness and the search for consciousness. Nash was not interested in any of the automatic techniques practised by the Surrealists and insisted, by contrast to what he believed to be the typical Surrealist standpoint, that he would not 'allow the promptings of the unconscious to lead me beyond a point of defensive control'.[49]

The second world war, far from being the 'massive intervention'[50] he had felt the first to be, found Nash as an artist fully prepared. His age and state of health made physical involvement impossible, and he never saw anything like Passchendaele – if anything existed – to throw his art onto a new course. His subject was aircraft, but he was not allowed to fly on account of his bronchial condition, and the great majority of his pictures show planes on the ground. Whereas in 1917 he needed a new direction, his major watercolours in the second war, which show crashed German aircraft in the English countryside, follow logically from the 1939 'Monster Field' in which dead trees had been metamorphosed into fallen aerial creatures. In the pictures of bombers Nash wanted to express his sense of insult at the hostile intrusion and show, in 'Bomber in the Wood' for instance, that, dominating though the machines might be when active, nature possessed the enduring power that would ultimately consume them.

Nash's authoritative picture of the second war, 'Totes Meer', is both a factual record and a summary of his feeling about death. The growth of its composition is documented in sketches made from photographs he took at Cowley dump of wrecked German aircraft near Oxford, which he described in a letter to Kenneth Clark, chairman of the War Artists' Advisory Committee: 'The thing looked to me suddenly, like a great inundating Sea. You might feel – under certain influences – a moonlight night for instance – this is a vast tide moving across the fields, the breakers rearing up and crashing on the plain. And then, no: nothing moves, it is not water or even ice, it is something static and dead. It is metal piled up, wreckage.'[51]

The scene is under the control of the moon, the same half moon that had threatened to draw the water over the pyramids in 'The Pyramids in the Sea'. In Nash's art this moon transmutes elements, shifts the balance between them, sets changes in motion. Water had always been dangerous, and in winter water can be hard as ice, which is inert and lifeless. The form of 'Totes Meer', the subject of wreckage, and Nash's hint in the letter to Clark that the waves might be ice, all relate it to Caspar David Friedrich's 'Arctic Shipwreck' (1824), a painting which interested the Surrealists for its metamorphic qualities. But even if it was consciously in Nash's mind, it could only have been for the way it complemented ideas already deeply rooted, because the winter sea in Nash's work belonged typically to Dymchurch, and the structure of 'Totes Meer', with its diagonal line cutting across the right side of the picture, is a Dymchurch one.

Nash has taken a low viewpoint on the subject, so that the horizon is high and not even the largest 'wave' breaks it, and a feeling is engendered that the whole event might be just below the ground. The turbid mass of wreckage spills into the light only in the top left-hand corner where the swell is strongest and the sea at one point meets the sky. There the wreckage *is* the sea, and works in the way it does in the Dymchurch picture 'The Sea', exerting through the sheer height of the waves a kind of pressure on the shore. Nash has interfused different images of death: the wreckage, the winter sea, the womb or cradle of the earth.

Nash first visited Madams, the home in Gloucestershire of Charles and Clare Neilson, in June 1938; it was to become a retreat for him from the anxiety and deprivations of the war and, together with the countryside around, was to be the most important source of material for pictures, other than ones of the war, until 1944. Nash's reversion to pure landscape, and until late 1942 to watercolour as a medium in preference to oil, seems like a defeat, a withdrawal when Surrealism was no longer meaningful and abstraction not a viable alternative. But his late landscape watercolours are a remarkable advance even on those of 1925, which mark the peak of his achievement in this area hitherto. From 1938 his pictures became increasingly relaxed, he worked more in terms of tonal gradation and intensity of colour which grew more vibrant as drawing became less important; some underdrawing in soft pencil or black chalk is usual to the end, but it was employed increasingly to briefly mark out the composition rather than to define forms. The 1944–5 watercolours from Cleeve Hill are immediate responses to nature comparable with the most vital and fluent landscapes of the twenties, but with less of the feeling that stylistic and technical problems are intervening between the subject and its realisation.

Nash no longer found what he wanted by exploring the individuality of places, the particulars of nature tend to be dissolved: individual and even grouped trees are not common; foregrounds, which link the painter most intimately with the subject, are sometimes abandoned altogether, and there is less descriptive drawing. This area of the Cotswold escarpment overlooking the Severn valley never became a 'place' for Nash, who was no longer looking for the visual features or historical associations that made an area unique. His friend Richard Seddon reported that Nash told him towards the end of his life that he wanted to cease trying to control nature,[52] and the almost abstract way in which the pools of colour form themselves seems to bear this out.

In November 1942 Nash first painted in the garden at Hilda Harrisson's house, Sandlands, at Boar's Hill outside Oxford, which looked over Bagley Woods towards Wittenham which Nash could see in the distance with the help of field glasses. The view of Wittenham conjured up memories of thirty years previously, and the play of sunlight and shade on the garden recalls the earliest landscape drawings like 'Bird Garden'. Commenting on his early work in a letter to his dealer Dudley Tooth in 1943, Nash remarked on how many of his first pictures had been night scenes, and added: 'Now I am re-opening my research – renewing the solution of the problem of light and dark and half-light.'[53] His research revolved round the changing seasons, and the ascendancy of sun or moon, with each solstice or equinox marking a new equation in the relationship between the two.

Within the framework of this scheme a remarkable development took place in Nash's actual painting, beginning with 'November Moon' which, with 'Sunflower and Sun', starts the series, and with its soft, spreading paint and balance of warm and cool colours, has a nostalgic and rather withdrawn character, and culminating in 'Landscape of the Vernal Equinox' and 'Landscape of the Moon's Last Phase' in which colour is rich and assertive and the materiality of the paint stressed. After 1943 Nash became less concerned with foreground, as he was also to be in his Cleeve Hill watercolours, and gradually he began painting landscapes that, because of their distance, were not seen – not, at least, with the naked eye – but imagined. Up to 1944, though some balance was always struck between the domains of the sun and moon, the moon was generally in the ascendant; after 'Landscape of the Moon's Last Phase' Nash's subject was the sun.

Nash's last oil paintings took up the sunflower theme he had investigated in the 1942 'Sunflower and Sun', but had not then pursued. 'Eclipse of the Sunflower' shows the flower's golden petals identifying with the sun which, for the moment, is all but hidden behind a dark disc, while the dying centre of the flower sinks back into the ground. It is a kind of casting off of material death while the sequel, 'Solstice of the Sunflower', realises the dynamic of a new life. Nash wrote of this: 'In the Solstice the spent sun shines from its zenith encouraging the sunflower in the dual role of sun and firewheel to perform its mythological purpose. The sun appears to be whipping the Sunflower like a top. The Sunflower Wheel tears over the hill cutting a path through the standing corn and bounding into the air as it gathers momentum. This is the blessing of the Midsummer Fire.'[54]

Nash's description was largely derived from his reading of Sir James Frazer's *The Golden Bough*, in particular the last two books, *Balder the*

Beautiful. For Frazer the killing of the legendary hero Balder was a mid-summer fertility ritual, his annual death representing the necessity for the sun to die and be reborn. Frazer explained that the old European custom of trundling a firewheel at the summer solstice meant that 'the sun, having now reached the highest point in the ecliptic, begins henceforward to descend',[55] and 'the custom of rolling a burning wheel down a hill, which is often observed at these ceremonies, might well pass for an imitation of the sun's course in the sky, and the imitation would be particularly appropriate on Midsummer Day when the sun's annual declension begins'.[56]

In 'Solstice of the Sunflower' the sun, on the decline after the midsummer, has placed its strength in the firewheel. Frazer said that as long as the wheel thrown from the top of the hill was still alight when it reached the valley below all was safe for the following year.[57] Nash's sunwheel bounds across the valley, and the red path that it traces through the corn is the blood of the sun which perpetuates fertility. It is not difficult to see why the Balder myth and the numerous crop fertility rituals practised by pastoral peoples which Frazer cites should have taken Nash's attention. Apart from his interest in the cycles of nature and the seasons and the more general equation of darkness and light, there was his preoccupation with continuity in the passing of authority through generations, which had manifested itself in his early 'acquisition' of Iver Heath by means of his drawings, and his emotional response to the illness and death of his father. Nash's handling of the theme was not confined to instances connected with his own family and its territory, but appears in many different forms, such as the notion of sacrifice and regeneration contained in 'We are Making a New World' and of renewal through surrender to a meta-phorical death in 'Harbour and Room'.

'Solstice of the Sunflower' relates directly to *The Golden Bough* and in this respect is an affirmation of the possibility of immortality. But it is also the culmination of the series begun in the autumn of 1942 when Nash first saw the distant view of Wittenham from the garden of Sandlands. Now Nash has not only approached the Clumps closer than ever before, he has also resolved the mystery contained within their dark copses by deforesting them. The imaginative invention of the imagery and the boldness of the colour witness his engrossment at the end of his life, when his health made painting for any length of time a strain, both in the act of painting itself and in the completion of a personal mythology. It is hard to envisage a more constructive response to the premonition of death than Nash's last paintings, in which sadness becomes exultation and death itself a celebration.

See bibliography for full details of works cited.

[1] *Outline*, pp.33–7.
[2] Reports of his progress at the Slade can be followed in his correspondence with his cousin Nell Bethell, his friend Mercia Oakley, and especially with Gordon and Emily Bottomley. See *Poet and Painter*, pp.12, 13, 15, 16.
[3] p.78.
[4] p.100.
[5] Letters of *c*.1 August 1912 and *c*.10 August 1912, *Poet and Painter*, pp.42 and 45.
[6] In his first letter to Nash, 14 April 1910, *Poet and Painter*, p.3. Nash twice reminded Bottomley of the advice he had given, in letters of 27 December 1913 and 23 August 1917, *Poet and Painter*, pp.67 and 86.
[7] pp.106–7.
[8] Untitled and undated, but early (*c*.1909), and the first line starts 'Night full of peace . . . .' It was written for Mercia Oakley when Nash was staying with family friends at Nunney Court, Frome.
[9] *Outline*, p.122.
[10] pp.131–3. Nash misspells Mundesley.
[11] *Outline*, pp.130 and 131.
[12] Letter of 21 August 1912, *Poet and Painter*, p.48.
[13] Letter of *c*. late July 1945, *Poet and Painter*, p.264.
[14] Letter of 18 April 1917, quoted in *Outline*, p.197.
[15] Letter of 2 March 1925.
[16] *Outline*, p.41
[17] In 'The New Generation', a review of an exhibition at the Independent Gallery, *The Athenaeum*, 11 February 1921.
[18] 'The London Group', *The Times*, 28 April 1928.
[19] Letter of 29 April 1928.
[20] Reported by William Gaunt, *Drawing and Design*, October 1926.
[21] In the introduction to *Paul Nash*, The Fleuron, 1927.
[22] Undated letter, *c*. November 1927.
[23] 'Memoir', p.37.
[24] Reported in Bertram, p.145.
[25] Undated letter.
[26] See *Outline*, p.222.
[27] According to Richard Seddon in 'Paul Nash 1889–1946', *Studio*, March 1948. Seddon talked to Nash just after his consultation with Horder in July 1945 and there is no reason to question the report. Bertram consulted Horder on the point when he was preparing his biography of Nash, and Horder rejected (letter of 14 May 1951, quoted in Bertram, p.269) the much-quoted rumour that Nash had been affected by gas in November 1917.
[28] 'Memoir', p.42.
[29] 'The Present Tendency of Paul Nash', by John Armstrong, *Apollo*, November 1932.
[30] Quoted in *Scandal and Parade. The Theatre of Jean Cocteau*, by Neal Oxenhandler, Constable, 1958, pp.90–91.
[31] 'Memoir', p.42.
[32] Information from Ruth Clark.
[33] 'The Jig of Forslin', 1916, part 2 of 'The Divine Pilgrim', *The Collected Poems of Conrad Aiken*, Oxford University Press, 1970, p.89.
[34] *Ushant. An Essay*, W. H. Allen, 1963, p.308.
[35] In an interview with William Gaunt in *Drawing and Design*, October 1926.
[36] In the introduction to his exhibition of watercolours at the Redfern Gallery, April 1937.
[37] Titled and dated photographs of oil paintings probably now destroyed indicate that Nash explored abstraction again briefly in 1933–4.
[38] In 'Picasso and Painting', *Weekend Review*, 27 June, and 'André Bauchant', *The Listener*, 3 June.
[39] Figures in one of Nash's three surviving notebooks (in the Tate Gallery Archive) show that he earned £1,191 from the sale of pictures in 1929–30 and £563 in 1931–2. The sums are probably net of commission.
[40] He wrote to Hilda Felce, 23 November 1931: 'Thank God I seem to be able to write, journalism is now my sole means of subsistence', and again to her on 23 January 1932: 'I haven't painted for months – just doing odd jobs and writing articles.'
[41] 'For, but not With', *Axis*, January 1935.
[42] Letter of 14 April 1934.
[43] *Dorset Shell Guide*, published in 1936.
[44] Nash wrote a perceptive review of the exhibition, 'Art and the English Press', *Weekend Review*, 17 June 1933.
[45] 'Picture History'.
[46] Ernst's article 'Les Mystères de la Forêt', *Minotaure*, 12 May 1934, shows that this is how he regarded the forest.
[47] 'Openings', *Signature*, July 1938.
[48] Letter, undated but *c*.12 July 1942. The author is grateful to Benedict Read for drawing his attention to it.
[49] 'The Life of the Inanimate Object', *Country Life*, 1 May 1937.
[50] Nash described it thus in 'Unit One', *The Listener*, 5 July 1933.
[51] Letter of 11 March 1941.
[52] 'Paul Nash 1889–1946', by Richard Seddon, *Studio*, March 1948.
[53] Undated letter, but October 1943.
[54] 'Picture History'.
[55] *The Golden Bough*, by James Frazer, abridged edition, Macmillan, 1959, p.622.
[56] ibid., p.643.
[57] ibid., p.705.

Paul Nash

A personal view of the man and the artist

The place of Paul Nash in the history of art during the first half of the present century appears, at first sight, difficult to determine. He was not an academic painter, working within the limits of the representational tradition, although much of the earlier phases of his art suggested that his loyalties would lie in that direction. At the same time, he cannot be identified with any of the experimental movements and revolutionary developments which emerged before, during and after the First World War, although he was not wholly uninfluenced by some of their aspects. The Post-Impressionists, the Cubists, the Futurists, the Expressionists, the Fauves, the Dadaists, the Constructivists, the Surrealists, and all the breakaway groups which stemmed from them, each made distinctive and easily identifiable contributions. But there always remained some important and highly individual painters and sculptors who, like Nash, were not prepared to accept the limitations which they felt to be imposed by adherence to any particular school or group, and their contribution can therefore only be assessed by some objective standard which can be applied with equal validity to the definition of art throughout the centuries.

If then, for the sake of argument, we may assume (as Paul Nash himself would have been ready to do) that art can be broadly defined as a means of communicating, in visual terms, those concepts, emotions and psychological responses which do not readily lend themselves to precise verbal description, we are in an altogether stronger position than if we were left to rely entirely upon our subjective reactions to the work before us.

Admittedly, an artist's work is necessarily conditioned to a large extent by his period, his nationality, his background and material circumstances, and does not depend solely upon his inherent genius. But if in art communication is a pre-requisite, there must be something worth communicating and it is here that the artist's personality and background come in. Is he someone whose concepts, emotions and psychological responses are worth communicating? Are we enriched by the depth of his experience? Are we moved by the sensitivity of his apprehension, enlightened by the acuteness of his observation, disturbed by the force of his reaction, diverted by the charm of his fantasy, warmed by the breadth of his humour? Has he the power, by the force of his insight, to continue to move us over the long divide of the years?

If we are fully to appreciate the quality of Paul Nash's contribution, and to acknowledge the extent to which (at his best) he realised many of these requirements, we must first consider how far his art was a true expression of himself. It has been said of him that he was essentially a poet and that his art was peculiarly English. Both claims are undoubtedly true and it is the qualities they describe which lend to his painting its particular validity.

The 'Englishness' of Nash's art expresses a quality which was, in the most precise sense, inherent in the man and sprang from his ancestry.

Notwithstanding Paul's finely chiselled aquiline features and his raven-black hair (strangely contrasting with the vivid blue of his piercing eyes), which carried a faint suggestion of some Mediterranean blood, his family on both sides was of pure English descent. His mother's people had been serving officers in the Royal Navy for at least four generations, and Nash himself was destined for a naval career and would have been sent for training to Dartmouth had he not been, as he later wrote, 'the kind of fool whose particular imbecility must prevent any success in a profession where accurate mathematical calculation is as essential as the breath of life'. His father's fore-bears had been yeoman farmers in North Buckingham, where they could be traced back to the early seventeenth century. A hundred years later their descendants were established as substantial landowners in the south of the county.

At Langley Rectory, an ample country house no longer in ecclesiastical occupation, Paul's formidable but genial grandfather still maintained the landowning tradition. 'Only at Langley something of the old state lingered', Nash wrote in *Outline*, 'Guests came and went, tea-parties gathered in the shade of the mulberry-tree, shooting luncheons were devoured in the paddock under the chestnuts, and Christmas was still a festival at Langley Rectory! That is something to remember from another age.'

It was indeed something to remember, and it left its indelible impress upon him. He remained a countryman at heart throughout his life. His periods of residence in London and Oxford, his visits to France, Spain, North Africa and, briefly, to the United States and Italy, never obscured his devotion to the English countryside, which he had come to know with that intimacy which springs from participation and understanding. He was not an outsider, gazing with a connoisseur's appreciation at lovely scenery, but a countryman, who accepts the natural interrelationship of landowner, farmer and tenant with the land they serve, and is instinctively involved in the rhythmic cycle of the seasons.

He had been born in London, on 11 May 1889, at Ghuznee Lodge, a rather forbidding Kensington house, the unlovable atmosphere of which he later described in the brilliantly witty and evocative opening passages of his un-finished autobiography. It was always an alien place to him, though he lived there with his barrister father, William Harry Nash and his mother Caroline, for twelve years, and it was there that his younger brother, John, and his sister Barbara were born. The family move, made for the sake of his mother, whose nervous ill-health was a cause of constant anxiety, must have been a profound relief to him, as the new house at Wood Lane, Iver Heath, was close to the familiar territory at Langley. He was still at St. Paul's School, Hammersmith, into which he had passed from the preparatory establishment of Colet Court. At both he had endured 'the complicated purgatory', described in *Outline*. Not only was uncontrolled bullying rife in the classes, but also at both schools he proved virtually impervious to teaching. For all his keen, lively and receptive intelligence, his real feeling for words, and considerable gifts of analysis and synthesis (perhaps inherited from his father) he was totally resistant to the teaching 'methods' then in vogue. Throughout his life he always found it difficult to be taught, though he could learn of his own accord with the greatest ease. The wide culture, the fund of information on a variety of subjects and the excellently balanced judgment which marked him in later life were therefore derived from his reading and from the circles in which he moved from the time of his childhood, and owed nothing to his formal 'education'. His very lack of co-ordinated instruction may well have operated to his advantage, because he always had to find his own way and was left free to give full play to his powerful imagination.

This advantage was certainly not apparent to his family when he left school without a single 'useful' qualification. It was essential that he should become self-supporting, but all enquiries about suitable 'openings' not unnaturally proved abortive and when it was suggested that he 'should go into a bank' Paul finally rebelled, and startled everyone by the sudden announcement that he was 'going to be an artist'. So, at the age of eighteen, he set about the business of acquiring some basic training, hampered as usual by his inability to benefit from formal teaching.

Up to this time he had displayed no especial inclination or aptitude for drawing, though he had amused his friends with some tenuous but lively caricatures and had indulged a passion for amateur theatricals by making models and producing scenery and costumes. His idea of an artistic career, according to his own account, was limited to becoming an illustrator and 'black-and-white' draughtsman. Although he was familiar with the clear, cool watercolours of Edward Lear, possessed by an aunt, and despite the fact that two members of his mother's family had been capable amateur painters, the thought of depicting the countryside he so much loved seems never to have occurred to him.

It may be that his romantic imagination had been fired by the idea of the poet-painter of popular fiction, for many of his youthful productions were derivative illustrations of the derivative verses at which he was trying his hand. Such youthful fancies were not, however, an adequate basis for a professional career, and he struggled to master the essential techniques, first at the Chelsea Polytechnic and then at the L.C.C. technical school in Bolt Court and, for a few terms, at the Slade. His work attracted notice from visiting professors, not because of its technical accomplishment, which was negligible, but because of the imaginative qualities which showed through its imperfections.

196 **November Moon** 1942 (entry on p.96)

230 **The Sun Descending** 1945 (entry on p.104)

233 **Eclipse of the Sunflower** 1946(?) (entry on p.104)

He received encouragement from Will (later Sir William) Rothenstein, and Gordon Bottomley, some of whose poems he had tried to illustrate, exerted a powerful early influence over him and became a life-long friend.

But it was Sir William Richmond, a then revered and ponderous academic painter and designer of mosaics, who, paradoxically, started Paul upon his future course. One day, while inspecting a handful of young Nash's newest attempts, he spotted the landscape background of one of the 'vision' drawings, and pronounced judgment – 'My boy, you should go in for Nature.' At first Paul did not appreciate the significance of this momentous utterance, but shortly afterwards, as he was strolling over the Oxfordshire hillsides near Wittenham Clumps, its full meaning struck him, and he began to draw those wooded hill-tops which were to haunt him for the rest of his life. From that moment he realised that he had come into his own. Like his forebears he would make his living from the land, not by tilling, but by painting it.

He now had confidence in himself and in the possibility of realising his ambitions. His first small exhibition at the Carfax Gallery, St. James's, attracted notice, and a year later, in 1914, an exhibition at the Dorien Leigh Gallery, held jointly with his brother John, won him a modest reputation as a promising and original young painter.

The originality lay in the complete freshness of his highly personal approach. He saw nature through his own eyes and was little if at all influenced by the work of other men. All the stored-up impressions of his childhood, temporarily obscured by his wretched schooldays and the second-hand romanticism of his adolescence, came to his aid. With an intimate understanding impossible to the town-dweller, he rendered the personality of the landscape and strove to embody in his work a realisation of some imminent force, some indwelling spirit, which could be sensed behind the surface appearance of the scene. When he had been very small, he had discovered, among the lofty elm-trees of Kensington Gardens, the magic of a 'Place', where 'the relationship of parts creates a mystery, an enchantment, which cannot be analysed', and that enchantment was to be with him for the rest of his life.

To the interpretation of the landscape he brought a poet's eye, for, having abandoned his literary ambitions, he now employed his poetic insight to seize the essence of the moment, arranging the elements of the actual landscape in such a way as to recreate his reactions to it. His technical mastery was as yet not always equal to the communication of his mood, so that, despite the evidence of his sensibility, we are often aware in these early watercolours that he is still groping for a technique which, when found, tends to become slightly mannered and over-elegant.

The elegance was rudely shattered by Nash's experience of war in the trenches. On the outbreak of the First World War he had married Margaret Theodosia Odeh, had enlisted in the Artists Rifles and been 'for home service only'. In 1916 he transferred to the Hampshire Regiment with the rank of Second Lieutenant, and in the following February was sent to Flanders. At first his drawings of the trenches and the country behind them were marked with much the same considered style he had applied to peaceful scenes at home. Then suddenly the manner changed. There was no time to bother with technique as he recorded the battle-front in every available moment. The sketches were exhibited as 'Drawings made in the Ypres Salient' in July 1917 while he was back in England, recovering from a lucky accident which saved him from the annihilation that overwhelmed his battalion at Hill 60. The show brought him immediate fame. Here at last was the horrifying truth about the devastated lands of Flanders. He was sent back to the front as Official War Artist and in feverish haste he recorded the full horror of the outraged 'Place' – 'Sunset and sunrise are blasphemous', he wrote, 'they are mockeries to man, only the black rain out of the bruised and swollen clouds or through the bitter black of night is fit atmosphere in such a land.'

Characteristically it was the fate of the land, even more than the sufferings of the men immersed in it, that had transformed him almost overnight from the promising artist into the great painter, employing the whole of his empathic powers to express the terrifying tragedy and to involve the beholder in a shared experience.

In 1919, having completed his large commissioned panels, 'The Menin Road' and 'Night Bombardment', Nash was faced with 'the struggles of a War Artist without a War'. The readjustment was not easy, but after a short period spent mostly in the Chilterns, he found Dymchurch and a new style. The wide horizons of the sea and shore bordering the Romney Marsh brought a fresh release of the spirit and he rendered the coast and the low lands behind it in a series of oils and watercolours of compelling insight. The human figure still occasionally appeared in his work, but, as in the war pictures, its role was entirely subsidiary to the main theme. Stylised figures of men in the trenches or serving the guns, of his wife and other women descending steps from the sea wall or pacing the empty promenade, do no more than provide a point of contrast, a visual focus in a landscape whose inner life is hidden from them. Stylised human figures were still retained in Nash's graphic work up to the early 'thirties and then they disappear. His occasional essays in portraiture, which had never been particularly successful, were likewise abandoned and 'The Place', imbued with what Anthony Bertram has aptly called the 'Presence of the Absent', was left to reign supreme. It has sometimes been suggested that this failure to come to terms with the human form must argue a certain coldness and aloofness in the painter himself. But such a contention is wholly unjustified. Those of us who knew Paul Nash intimately were always aware of the exceptional warmth and generosity of his character. His wit was keen and sometimes sardonic, but it was never malicious and any conversation in which he took part rippled with a laughter generated by the gaiety and humour of his repartee. His kindness to his friends and fellow artists was proverbial. Human relationships always meant a great deal to him, a fact to which his serious or playful letters, often enlivened by caricatures of himself and others, bear abundant witness. He wrote exactly as he talked, and the flavour of his conversation can be recaptured in many published letters. He delighted in good company, good food, and good wine, and his immaculate, rather ambassadorial appearance and debonair manners merited for him the title accorded by one of his friends – 'the last civilised man'.

After five years spent largely at Dymchurch, he and his wife moved to Iden in 1925 and then, after some time spent in southern France, to Rye in 1930 where he was stricken with his first attack of the severe cardiac asthma which worsened as the years went on and finally led to his premature death in 1946, at the age of fifty-seven. In face of this appalling handicap, which towards the end so weakened him that at times he was unable to paint, he had need of all his courage and gaiety. He never abandoned either his hope of partial recovery or his determination to work, and the physical suffering, which left its trace on his features, ennobled rather than embittered his character.

The 'discovery of the Megaliths' at Avebury followed his departure from Rye in 1932. The Nashes then spent the next three years largely at Swanage and in 1936 they settled in a house at Hampstead. The 'settlement' was of short duration, for with the imminent threat of another war, they realised that Paul's rapidly deteriorating health would make him a liability in London, and they moved to Oxford in the later summer of 1939.

The restrictions imposed on his movements by his recurrent illness, when added to the difficulties and frustrations of war-time travel, limited the personal contacts with his older friends, which had always meant so much to him. But nothing daunted, he kept up with them as best he could by letter, and at Oxford, where his charm and wit made him a welcome guest at the High Tables of several colleges, a new and devoted circle of friends grew up round him. His work as an Official War Artist brought him to London at fairly regular intervals for meetings at the Ministries of Aviation and Information, and he used these opportunities to see old friends and make new ones.

It was on such a visit in 1941, when he gave a lecture on Surrealism at Morley College, that E. H. Ramsden and I first encountered him personally (though we had corresponded before). Our friendship rapidly quickened into a great mutual understanding, stimulated in the first place partly by Paul's enthusiasm for the project of the *New Movements in Art – Contemporary Work in England* exhibition, which we arranged at the London Museum in the spring of 1942. He welcomed the chance of showing a few of his own watercolours and collages beside the work not only of old friends like Nicholson, Hepworth and Moore, but of younger and still unknown contemporaries, in whose struggles for recognition he always showed a genuine and sympathetic interest. Even later, undeterred by the memory of the rapid disintegration of Unit One, the loose-knit group of experimental artists he had initiated in 1932, he was toying with the idea of a new group for younger artists which should be, as he told us, 'a nucleus – a nucleus with antennae'.

[43]

The vivid phrase was typical of his remarkable power to raise up in the minds of his hearers the same visual image which was in his own, and it was this elegant economy in the choice of the right word which made him a brilliant raconteur. In the Acland Nursing Home at Oxford, for instance, when he was recovering from a severe attack of pneumonia early in 1944, he entertained us with a lively account of a provincial French music-hall, of which the principal scene had centred round an *urinoire*, in which, their heads and feet being exposed to view, the occupants were constantly hindered from their business by having to doff their hats and greet the passing ladies whom they recognised. Propped up against his pillows, with one hand resting on a small raffia mat he had 'imported' to relieve the clinical austerity of the room, Paul recreated the scene so incisively that we felt ourselves transported back over ten or fifteen years to see it through his eyes.

The descriptive phrase was never lacking. The London Museum, to which he sometimes came to take a glass of sherry with us, he called 'the highest sounding dive in London', and on one occasion, when we were dining with him and his wife at the Russell Hotel, where they used to stay, he solemnly assured us that, if we heard a rattle of musketry, there would be no cause for alarm – it would merely be his new denture and not the start of an air raid. His delight in fanciful conceits and in schoolboy puns, as well as in the more sophisticated forms of word-play, made his letters a constant, though often very long-awaited, pleasure. Knowing that I had taken part in the excavations at Maiden Castle in his favourite county of Dorset, he sent me, after a long delay in which we had anxiously looked for news of him, one of his own perceptive photographs of two Iron-Age skeletons, apparently deep in conversation in their double grave at the gateway of the great hill-fort, with a couple of apologetic lines, saying that he had intended the offering as a Christmas card, but that it had 'crash-landed on the wrong side of Easter'.

The gesture and the wording were characteristic, combining as they did the courteous remembrance of a friend's professional interests with an expression of his own. For the Maiden Castle skeletons, no less than the pieces of twisted driftwood, the wooden egg-crate, the curiously-wrought ivory bobbins, the shells and dried seaweed, all formed part of that 'collection' of *objets trouvés* to which (stored in his memory or recorded by his camera) the great prehistoric monoliths of Avebury and the fallen tree-trunks in a Gloucestershire field also belonged. They added a poignancy and provided a focus for many of his later studies in oils and watercolour of landscapes which achieved the status of being 'Places'. In the earlier work his sense of the *genius loci*, the indwelling spirit of the place, is implicit in the general mystery of the scene, but later it is often, as it were, embodied and represented by one of the Found Objects, which lend a particular significance to the scene. This significance is sometimes magic and prehistoric, for Nash was always fascinated by curious lore and legend, whether propounded by seventeenth and eighteenth-century antiquarians like Sir Thomas Browne and Stukeley, or by more scientifically-minded nineteenth-century anthropologists like Frazer. The incorporation of their ideas into his pictures frequently took on a surrealist form, expressed by the inclusion of the appropriate 'object'. But, although Nash had participated in the Surrealist Exhibition in London in 1936 and had been hailed by no less an authority than René Magritte as 'The Master of the Object', his images were rarely if ever 'laid' in the strictly surrealist sense. Some of his compositions undoubtedly originated in dreams, or sprang from the free association of ideas or from actually observed haphazard juxtapositions. But more often, as I have suggested, the perceived sense of the *genius loci* was deliberately interpreted by the introduction of a Found Object.

This difference of approach emphasises the fact that Paul Nash never fully identified himself with any of the experimental movements, for reasons which he explained in an essay entitled 'For but not With', contributed to *Axis* in 1935, after the break-up of the Unit One group. Apart from his sturdy English independence, which prevented him from either founding or following any 'school', he felt an innate distrust of the doctrinaire solemnity usually associated with such movements. He himself was immensely serious and professional in his attitude to his work, but he was never in the least solemn about it – or about anything else, for that matter. His feeling for the symbolism which he detected in Places and Objects was completely genuine, but his wit and sense of fun were always breaking in, so that some piece of nonsense which is endowed with real 'significance' in one picture, will turn up in another as a joke. He himself derived immense amusement from the solemn Freudian or Jungian meaning read into some of his works – 'Jam for the Psycho Boys', as he said to a friend, when looking at *Nocturnal Landscape.*

In the final phase, however, he treated his own symbolism more seriously. His appointment as Official Artist to the Royal Air Force had given him a new inspiration, since his attention was already turning from the earth to the air. Owing to his physical condition he was never allowed to fly, but notwithstanding this disadvantage, he rendered the feeling of planes in flight or on the ground, in triumph or in defeat, with an unerring empathy which won enthusiastic acclaim from the men who flew them, although it was not invariably so well received by the brass hats on the ground. But for him the true denizens of the sky were not the planes. His imagination was filled with the cosmic interplay of sun and moon and with the effects of rain and mist, frost and snow, sunshine and cloud shadow as they moved across the wide landscape. In place of the sun he set the sunflower in the sky, to rise, to reach its solstice and to be eclipsed. The release was complete. 'Death, about which we are all thinking, death, I believe, is the only solution to this problem of how to be able to fly. Personally, I feel that if death can give us that, death will be good.'

Few painters of his generation had a greater ability than Paul Nash to leave upon the beholder the deep imprint of his own heightened perception, whether grave or gay. We are enriched by his shared experience of the land, the sea and the sky, and are caught into a world of sharpened awareness because we have seen through his eyes. There is no 'correct' way to look at his pictures, no 'orthodox' interpretation of their meaning. Even when the painter himself sought, as he sometimes did, to offer some explanation, he was at pains to emphasise that he was not pronouncing a dogma, but making a tentative suggestion. To most of us who have devoted close study to his work, his paintings and drawings convey a sense of the deep sincerity of Nash's approach to nature and of his abiding belief in an underlying unity, expressed in the 'Spirit of the Place'. At his finest he attained great heights of lyricism, and his personal contribution to European art, marked as it is by a rare degree of insight, will remain a witness, not only to his own individuality, but also to the quality of the English genius in the first half of the twentieth century.

Catalogue

The works are listed in chronological order. Measurements are given in the order: height, width, and (where applicable) depth. Details of medium are as complete as is known. Oil paintings are on canvas and watercolours on paper except where otherwise stated. Where several media are used the order 'watercolour, ink, chalk, pencil' is followed regardless of the quantity of each.

The earliest known catalogued exhibition at which each picture was shown is given in the catalogue, followed by the number at the 1948 Memorial Exhibition at the Tate, if the picture was shown there. The List of Exhibitions is chronological and the abbreviations used in the catalogue entries are explained there. Minor mixed exhibitions are referred to only in the catalogue, with details of the month and year in which they were shown, and are not included in the List of Exhibitions.

Details of books referred to in the catalogue are listed in the Bibliography.

Where references are made in notes to dates attributed to pictures by the artist or Margaret Nash, those by Paul Nash are usually on the backs of photographs of the pictures or in the two display volumes of photographs of his work which he kept, and those by Margaret Nash are from the photographs of her husband's pictures which she presented to the Victoria and Albert Museum Library.

Abbreviations used in the catalogue (other than exhibition titles) are:
- s. signed 'Paul Nash' (any different form of signature is detailed)
- d. dated
- l. lower or left
- r. right
- * following the title indicates that the work is reproduced

1 **Angel and Devil*** 1910(?)
Watercolour, ink and pencil, $14 \times 10\frac{1}{2}$ in.
Monogram l.l.
Exh: OAC 1931 (11)
Victoria and Albert Museum, London

3

4

Nash wrote an accompanying poem on the same sheet, and though he later removed this and destroyed it, a manuscript version of the poem survives:

A place of gibbet-shapen trees & black abyss
Where gaunt hills brooded dark & evil
Girdled by dense wet woods & rushing streams
A dread place only seen in dreams
Of which there is no history but this
That on yon' stony tor
An angel fought a devil.

Nash's early letters to Gordon Bottomley show that Bottomley had seen it by April 1910. It is also titled 'The Combat' in early letters.

2   Our Lady of Inspiration* 1910
Ink and chalk, 9 × 6¾ in. Monogram l.r.
Exh: Newcastle 1971 (2)
Tate Gallery, London

Frontispiece to a book of nine handwritten poems by Nash, dedicated 'To Mary' (Sybil Fountain) and dated 11 May 1910. The title is inscribed on the opposite page.

3   A Lane in Blue* 1910
Chalk and pencil, 13⅝ × 9¾ in. s. & d. 1910 l.r.
Exh: Carfax 1912 (8)
Miss Barbara Nash

Made when Nash was staying with relatives at Yately, Hampshire. The signature and date appear to be in a later handwriting of Nash, but are probably correct.

4   Bird Garden* 1911
Watercolour, ink and chalk, 15¼ × 13¼ in.
Monogram l.l., inscribed with title and monogram on the mount, and d. August 1911 on the back
Exh: Carfax 1912 (2); Tate 1948 (69)
National Museum of Wales, Cardiff

In his autobiography, *Outline*, Nash makes it clear that this was his first successful drawing of the part of the garden at Iver Heath which he called the bird garden.

5   Night in Bird Garden 1911(?)
Watercolour, ink and chalk, 20½ × 17 in. s. & d. 1911 l.r.
Exh: Carfax 1912 (6); Tate 1948 (71)
Private collection

Nash wrote to the first owner, Mrs George Mortimer, in April 1945: 'I think its awfully good! I have been studying the technique which I had forgotten, and

as I looked closely into the drawing all my early life of those days and nights came creeping back into memory and I remembered the sensation of doing that drawing of the night shrubs and trees and how I wanted to give the true feeling of a nocturnal scene and must get the sky that elusive colour – that luminous darkness.' The picture has always been dated 1912, but the inscribed date of 1911, though it was added together with the signature at Mrs Mortimer's request in August 1931, and is not, therefore, firm evidence, seems likelier on grounds of style.

6   Vision at Evening 1911
Watercolour, chalk and pencil, $7\frac{1}{8} \times 13\frac{7}{8}$ in.
Monogram l.r.
Exh: Newcastle 1971 (3)
Victoria and Albert Museum, London

Nash describes making the picture in *Outline* (p.105, but it is not referred to by title), and it is clear that it was made in the spring of 1911 at Prestwood in the Chilterns.

7   The Wanderer* 1911(?)
Watercolour, ink, chalk and pencil, $18\frac{1}{2} \times 14$ in.
Monogram l.r.
Exh: Carfax 1912 (15)
Trustees of the British Museum, London

8   The Falling Stars 1911–12(?)
Watercolour, ink, chalk and pencil, $12\frac{1}{2} \times 9$ in.
Unsigned
Exh: Carfax 1912 (3)
Sir John and Lady Rothenstein

Gordon Bottomley rebuked Nash in a letter of 19 August 1912 for the violence of his technique in this drawing: 'You should not dig out stars and moons with a knife.' Nash described his method (21 August): 'The back ground of the star drawing is blue ink first, then chalk, then Indian ink then conté and the holes & scars are the places where a moon, some too many stars, two embracing figures, & a fairy have been not quite successfully obliterated. I don't generally behave like this but this is an unfortunate case.' The drawing was bought at the Carfax show by Nash's most important early champion, William Rothenstein, and it was probably the first picture Nash sold other than to members of the family and their friends. It is sometimes dated 1911, and may have been begun then, but the Bottomley correspondence shows it is mainly a work of 1912.

9   The Peacock Path 1912
Watercolour, ink and chalk, $18 \times 14\frac{3}{4}$ in.
Monogram l.r. and inscribed with title beneath
Exh: Carfax 1912 (19); Tate 1948 (72)
Benedict Read

10   The Pyramids in the Sea* 1912
Watercolour, ink and chalk, $12\frac{3}{4} \times 11\frac{1}{2}$ in. s.l.r.
and inscribed 'Mercia from Paul' on the mount
Exh: Carfax 1912 (5); Tate 1948 (74)
Tate Gallery, London

Nash recorded making the drawing in a letter to Bottomley of 21 August 1912, where he referred to 'a queer drawing of pyramids crashing about in the sea in uncanny eclipsed moonlight'.

11   The Three 1912(?)
Watercolour, ink and chalk, $15\frac{1}{8} \times 10\frac{5}{8}$ in.
Monogram l.r. and inscribed with title on the mount
Exh: LG August 1959 (4)
Anthony d'Offay Gallery, London

The subject is the row of elms that bounded the garden of the Nashes' home at Iver Heath; see also No.22.

12   Under the Hill* 1912
Watercolour and ink, $15\frac{1}{2} \times 12\frac{1}{4}$ in.
Monogram l.r.
Exh: Carfax 1912 (16)
Carlisle Art Gallery

Drawn near the Thames close to Wittenham when Nash was staying with relatives at Sinodun in September 1912. He had written to Bottomley, 21 August 1912: 'I am going to Wallingford in Berkshire next month and there hope to find some fine things [,] those wonderful downs and wild woods by the river I have haunted them often and now I am going to try & interpret some of their secrets.' See also No.13 which dates from the same time.

13   The Wood on the Hill* 1912
Watercolour, ink and chalk, $13\frac{1}{2} \times 13$ in.
Monogram l.r.
Exh: Carfax 1912 (11)
Dr and Mrs Martin Cardew

A drawing of Wittenham Clumps from the same time as No.12, and a similar view to No.23.

14   The Cliff to the North* 1912–13
Watercolour, ink and chalk with white heightening, $15 \times 11\frac{1}{2}$ in.
Unsigned, but s. twice and monogrammed and inscribed with title on the original mount
Exh: DL 1913 (22); Tate 1948 (75)
Fitzwilliam Museum, Cambridge

Generally dated 1913, but the trip to Norfolk on which it was made, or at least begun, was in December 1912, and in a letter to Rothenstein (undated, but 1913) Nash referred to it as 'made about last Christmas'. It is described as 'new' in an undated letter to Bottomley of January 1913 (but mistakenly thought to be of November 1912 in the published correspondence, *Poet and Painter*, letter 57). The left-hand monogram and the 'Paul' of the signature

13

on the mount appear to be in a later hand of Nash, and could have been added at the time of the 1945 Cheltenham exhibition.

15   Lavengro and Isopel in the Dingle*
1912–13
Watercolour, ink and pencil, 18¼ × 14½ in.
s. Nash and monogram l.r.
Exh: DL 1913 (21); Tate 1948 (73)
Tate Gallery, London

The subject was taken from George Borrow's *Lavengro* (1851). The models were Nash's friend Mercia Oakley and his fellow student from the Slade, Rupert Lee, and the setting was Richmond Park. Various letters, to Mercia Oakley, Gordon Bottomley and William Rothenstein, show that it was begun in March 1912 and abandoned in April, revived and sent to Bottomley for his advice later that year, and further worked upon in the autumn of 1913. A study for the figures (d. 1911 but in a later hand of Nash) is also in the collection of the Tate.

16   Night Landscape 1912–14
Watercolour, ink, chalk and pencil, 14½ × 12 in.
Unsigned
Exh: DL 1913 (20)
Arts Council of Great Britain

The Nash-Bottomley correspondence (allowing for the misdating of letter 57, see No.14) suggests it was begun at the end of 1912 or very early in 1913. It was shown at the Dorien Leigh Gallery with the title 'The Archer', and the second date of 1914, which has always been associated with the picture, probably refers to the year the figure of the archer was expunged – though it is still faintly visible.

17   A Dawn* 1913(?)
Watercolour and pencil, 10 × 8 in. Unsigned
Mrs Oliver Woods

The title and date of this picture, which was unrecorded before being given away by the artist shortly before his death, were given by Margaret Nash; she also said it was shown at the Dorien Leigh exhibition, though it was certainly not catalogued. The date is uncertain and could be earlier.

18   A Drawing 1913
Watercolour, ink and chalk, 22 × 15 in. s. Nash and monogram l.r.
Exh: DL 1913 (3)
W. R. Brinton

An Iver Heath landscape.

12

14

15

17

19 In a Garden under the Moon 1913
Watercolour, ink and pencil, $13\frac{3}{4} \times 9\frac{3}{4}$ in.
Monogram l.r. and inscribed with title beneath
Private collection

The picture's first owner was Mrs Madge Kendal Lee who shared a flat with Margaret Nash before her marriage, and herself married Paul's friend Rupert Lee. Nash told her that it was an illustration to Coleridge's poem 'Christabel'. But the scene appears to show Salome dancing before Herod, with a scene on the right with a man wielding a dagger, which might be connected with the beheading of St. John the Baptist. Its only obvious relation to 'Christabel' is that it is – like several of Nash's early subjects – a moonlit night scene. At a time when Nash was intrigued by the power of darkness and the lure of the feminine he might have been drawn to the stories both of Christabel and Salome, and if it was Oscar Wilde's *Salome* he had particularly in mind, he would have recognised the essential thematic role played by the moon in the development of the drama.

20 William Harry Nash, the artist's father
1913
Watercolour and pencil, $11\frac{1}{8} \times 8\frac{1}{2}$ in.
Monogram and s. Nash and d. June 1913 top r.
Victoria and Albert Museum, London

21 Margaret Odeh 1913
Watercolour and pencil, 19×13 in.
Inscribed 'Bunty Margaret 1913' l.l.
Private collection

22 The Three in the Night* 1913
(repr. on p.9)
Watercolour, ink and chalk, $20\frac{3}{4} \times 13\frac{1}{2}$ in.
Unsigned
Exh: DL 1913 (5); Tate 1948 (76)
Private collection

The subject is similar to No.11. The picture was originally signed, but the edges have been reduced as a result of damage.

23 Wittenham Clumps 1913(?)
Watercolour, ink and chalk, $12\frac{1}{8} \times 15\frac{5}{8}$ in.
s. Nash and monogram l.r.
Exh: ? Friday Club February 1914 (38) as
'Castle Hill'
Carlisle Art Gallery

Margaret Nash dated it 1911–12 which seems too early on grounds of style. The suggestion that it was shown at the Friday Club in February 1914 was made under the reproduction in *Poet and Painter*, and is probably right, but the date given there of 1914 seems unlikely, since Nash generally visited Wittenham in the autumn, and was certainly there in September 1913. A similar view to No.13.

JOHN AND PAUL NASH

24 Poster for their joint exhibition at the Dorien Leigh gallery 1913
Oil and sealing wax, 21¾ × 16½ in.
Private collection
In a letter to Margaret Odeh of 4 November 1913, ten days before the opening of the joint exhibition, Nash wrote that John and he were 'jointly creating the poster, which is great fun. We are painting it in oil and cieling [sic] wax and it comes on fine'. The poster shows Paul (left) and John Nash in the foreground and, against the background of Wittenham Clumps, Rupert Lee and his future wife Madge (see No.19), Margaret Odeh and, probably, the painter's sister Barbara.

28

25 Avenue 1914
Watercolour, ink and pencil, 14½ × 11½ in. s.l.l.
Exh: Redfern 1961 (2)
Private collection
A close-up view of the trees in the orchard at Silverdale seen in No.29. See also the note to No.27.

26 The Elms 1914
Watercolour, ink and chalk, 26 × 18½ in. s.l.r.
Exh: ?Whitechapel 1914 (185) as 'Landscape in Buckinghamshire' (lent by Edward Marsh, the first owner of this picture); Tate 1948 (77)
Walker Art Gallery, Liverpool
An Iver Heath landscape.

29

27 The Monkey Tree 1914
Watercolour, ink and pencil on tracing paper, 15 × 17¾ in. Monogram l.l.
Exh: London Group March 1915 (38)
Victoria and Albert Museum, London
The view is from the front of Bottomley's house, The Sheiling, Silverdale near Carnforth, Lancashire, which overlooked Morecambe Bay. Nash and his fiancée stayed there in July 1914. A second slightly different version without the figure (14½ × 18½ in. Private collection) was probably derived from this one, and was shown at the 1917 Birmingham exhibition (dated 1916 in the Birmingham catalogue).

Nash reported to William Rothenstein that, as a result of the trip to Bottomley's and then to the Lake District, he had 'the beginnings of no less than 26 drawings' (14 September 1914). They include this one, Nos.25, 29, 30, 31.

28 Nude, Iver Heath* 1914
Watercolour, ink and chalk, $11\frac{1}{2} \times 9$ in. s. & d. 1914 l.r.
Exh: ?Cheltenham 1945 (51b) as 'Figure Study'
Private collection
A drawing of Margaret Odeh, who gave it this title; it has also been called 'Margaret in the Garden, Iver Heath'.

29 Orchard* 1914
Watercolour, ink and chalk, $14\frac{1}{2} \times 16\frac{1}{2}$ in. s.l.r.
Exh: London Group November 1916 (77)
Osborne Robinson, O.B.E.
The orchard was at Bottomley's Lancashire home; see Nos.25 and 27.

30 Summer Landscape* 1914
Watercolour, ink and chalk, $19\frac{3}{4} \times 14\frac{7}{8}$ in.
Unsigned
The Lord Goodman, C.H.
Probably a Silverdale landscape; see No.27.

31 Thirlmere* 1914
Watercolour, ink and chalk, $14 \times 14\frac{3}{4}$ in. s. Nash and monogram l.l.
Exh: NEAC winter 1914 (241)
Birmingham City Museums and Art Gallery
See No.27.

32 The Cherry Orchard (?)* 1917
Watercolour, ink and chalk, $22\frac{1}{4} \times 18\frac{1}{2}$ in.
s. Nash and monogram l.r.
Exh: London Group November 1917 (76)
Tate Gallery, London
The identification of the watercolour on exhibition with the picture of this title shown at the London Group is not certain, but the subject of the watercolour is certainly cherry trees, and the style and mood fit the date as well as can be calculated on the basis of the very few pictures other than war ones that exist from the years 1915–17. 'The Cherry Orchard' was made at John Drinkwater's home, Winston's Cottage, Far Oakridge, Gloucestershire, where Nash went in July 1917, partly to plan the exhibition that Drinkwater arranged for him at the Birmingham Repertory Theatre in September. In a

30

31

32

letter of 26 July, after the visit, Nash told Drink-water that he was submitting the picture to the London Group. In July 1917 Nash had recovered from his injury at the front in May, but did not yet know that his return to the front would be in the privileged role of an official artist. This might help to account for the extraordinarily tense imagery of the picture which seems more a late winter than a summer design.

33   Chaos Decoratif* 1917
Watercolour, ink and pencil, $10\frac{1}{4} \times 7\frac{3}{4}$ in.
Unsigned
Exh: Goupil 1917 (1)
City of Manchester Art Galleries
This and 'The Front Line. St. Eloi' (No.34) belong to the March–May period of Nash's service at the front.

33

34 The Front Line. St. Eloi 1917
Watercolour, ink and chalk, 8¾ × 8 in. Unsigned
Exh: Goupil 1917 (15); Tate 1948 (82)
Victoria and Albert Museum, London
Also known as 'Old Front Line. St Eloi' and 'St Eloi.
The Ypres Salient'. Early photographs show that it
was originally signed 'Nash' l.r. before the addition
of black chalk there. See No.33.

35 Dumbarton Lakes 1917–18
Watercolour, ink and chalk with white
heightening on brown paper, 10 × 14 in.
Unsigned
Exh: LG 1918 (17)
National Gallery of Canada, Ottawa
Used as a study for 'The Mule Track' (No.44). This
drawing and Nos.36, 37 and 39–43 date from Nash's
service as an official artist at the front, and were,
therefore, begun in November-December 1917. Nash
began at least sixty drawings on the battlefields which
he worked up after returning home; so those shown
here are all dated 1917–18. But six of the most important, including this one, Nos.39 and 41, were
reproduced in *Country Life*, 15 January 1918, so
must have been substantially complete by the end of
1917, and it is possible that all were.

36 The Field of Passchendaele 1917–18
Watercolour, ink and chalk, 9⅝ × 13⅝ in.
Unsigned
City of Manchester Art Galleries
See No.35.

37 Landscape. Year of Our Lord, 1917 1917–18
Watercolour, ink and chalk with white
heightening on brown paper, 10½ × 14 in.
Unsigned
Exh: LG 1918 (4)
National Gallery of Canada, Ottawa
See No.35.

38 The Menin Road 1918
Watercolour, ink and chalk, 16 × 22¾ in.
s. P Nash l.l.
Exh: LG 1918 (48)
Trustees of the Imperial War Museum, London
Study for a large section of the oil of the same title
(No.47).

39 Nightfall. Zillebecke District* 1917–18
Chalk on brown paper, 10¼ × 14 in. Unsigned
Exh: LG 1918 (37); Tate 1948 (88)
Trustees of the Imperial War Museum, London
See No.35.

39

40 Ruined Country. Old Battlefield, Vimy*
1917–18 (repr. on p.10)
Watercolour and chalk, 11 × 15¼ in. Unsigned
Exh: LG 1918 (2)
Trustees of the Imperial War Museum, London
See No.35.

41 Sunrise. Inverness Copse 1917–18
Watercolour, chalk and ink on brown paper,
9¾ × 13¾ in. Unsigned
Exh: LG 1918 (38)
Trustees of the Imperial War Museum, London
Used as a study for 'We are Making a New World'
(No.46). See also No.35.

42 Vimy Ridge 1917–18
Watercolour, ink and chalk, 10½ × 14 in.
Unsigned
Exh: LG 1918 (12)
Dr P. D. Bennett
See No.35.

43

43 Vimy Ridge* 1917–18
Watercolour, 10 × 14 in. s. & d. 1917 l.r.
*Atkinson Art Gallery, Southport (Merseyside
Metropolitan District of Sefton)*
See No.35.

44 The Mule Track 1918
Oil, 24 × 36 in. s.l.r.
Exh: Morley College 1971 (11)
Trustees of the Imperial War Museum, London
A commission from the Ministry of Information
based on the design of 'Dumbarton Lakes' (No.35).

45

45 Void* 1918
Oil, 28 × 36 in. s. & d. 1918 mid r.
Exh: LG 1918 (54)
National Gallery of Canada, Ottawa

46 We are Making a New World* 1918
Oil, 28 × 36 in. Unsigned
Exh: LG 1918 (29)
Trustees of the Imperial War Museum, London
Based on the design of 'Sunrise. Inverness Copse'
(No.41).

47 The Menin Road 1918–19
Oil, 72 × 125 in. s. & d. 1919 l.l.
Exh: RA 1919 (74); Tate 1948 (2)
Trustees of the Imperial War Museum, London
Nash received the commission for the picture, which was originally to have been called 'A Flanders Battlefield', in April 1918, and worked on it between June and February 1919. He recorded that the scene was near Gheluvelt in the Tower Hamlets district. Preparatory drawings exist in the Imperial War Museum (No.38) and the National Gallery of Canada.

48 Wire* 1918–19
Watercolour, ink and chalk, 18¾ × 24½ in. s. & d. 1918. 1919 l.r.
Exh: RA 1919 (182)
Trustees of the Imperial War Museum, London
Correspondence between Nash and the Ministry of Information in the Imperial War Museum shows that the picture, which is also known as 'Wire, Hindenburg Line', was substantially complete towards the end of 1918. Nash intended to make a lithograph from the design, but did not do so.

49 A Night Bombardment 1919–20
Oil, 72 × 84 in. s. & d. 1920 l.r.
National Gallery of Canada, Ottawa
Based on a drawing of the same title shown at Nash's 1918 Leicester Galleries exhibition (53). A letter to Gordon Bottomley of 30 May 1919 (not published in *Poet and Painter*), shows that Nash was then about to start the picture, which was a commission from the Canadian War Records. It was Nash's final first-world-war picture.

50 The Field Path 1918
Watercolour and chalk, 10 × 10¾ in. s. & d. 1918 l.l. and inscribed on the mount 'Gordon Bottomley from Paul Nash 1921' and 'for the plays'
Exh: Newcastle 1971 (11)
Carlisle Art Gallery
A gift from Nash to Bottomley in exchange for books of Bottomley's plays and poems.

51 Sudden Storm* 1918 (repr. on p.10)
Watercolour, chalk and pencil, 11 × 15½ in. s. & d. 1918 l.l.
Exh: OAC 1931 (10); Tate 1948 (89)
Mr and Mrs William Crabtree

Nash wrote on the back of a photograph 'drawing in the Chilterns just before the Armistice'. He was sharing a studio with his brother John at Chalfont St. Peter, and the view is the same as in John Nash's 1918 oil 'The Cornfield' (coll: Tate Gallery).

52 Barbara Nash *c.*1914
Watercolour, ink and pencil, 16½ × 13 in. s. and monogram l.l.
John Nash, C.B.E., R.A.

53 Margaret Nash *c.*1919–21
Watercolour and pencil, 10 × 8 in.
Inscribed 'Margaret Dymchurch 1921' top l.
Private collection
The date appears to have been altered by Margaret Nash, but it is more likely to be of the early Dymchurch years than of 1914, which is the date given by Margaret for the reproduction in *Outline*.

54 The Chilterns 1919
Watercolour and ink, 11 × 15 in. s. & d. 1919 mid r. and d. 1919 l.r.
Castle Howard collection
A Chiltern landscape, probably the same as No.58.

55 Night Tide 1919
Watercolour, ink and chalk, 11 × 15¼ in. s. & d. 1919 l.r.
Exh: Fitzroy Street 1919 (26)
Trustees of the British Museum, London

56 The Sea Wall* 1919
Watercolour, ink and chalk, 11 × 15 in. s.l.l.
Exh: Fitzroy Street 1919 (27)
Private collection

57 The White Woods 1919
Watercolour and pencil, 10¾ × 15⅛ in. s. & d. 1919 l.r.
Exh: Fitzroy Street 1919 (18)
National Gallery of Victoria, Melbourne
The woods were at Whiteleaf, Buckinghamshire.

58 Windy Hill* 1919
Watercolour and pencil, 11¼ × 15¼ in. s. & d. 1919 l.l.
Sir Antony and Lady Hornby
Probably a Chiltern landscape, the same as No.54.

56

58

61

59   White Cross 1920
Watercolour, ink and pencil, 14¾ × 10¾ in.
s. & d. 1920
Exh: London Group May 1920 (95)
Castle Howard collection
Whiteleaf Cross was a favourite subject, which Nash
painted till 1935. See also No.128.

60   Chiltern Hills *c.*1920
Oil, 20 × 24 in. s.l.l.
Exh: ? NEAC June 1920 (90), this title
Plymouth City Museum and Art Gallery

61   The Steps* 1920–23
Oil, 20 × 24 in. s. & d. 1920–23 mid.l.
Piccadilly Gallery, London
The crisp, dry handling of the sea area is in keeping
with the later date on the picture, while the more
agitated treatment of the steps is typical of the earlier
date. The female figure on the sea wall and steps is
found otherwise only in pictures up to 1922 (cf.
Nos.69 and 70), and it is most unlikely that the
figure was added at the later date.

62   Whiteleaf Orchard* *c.*1920–21
Oil, 20 × 24 in. s.l.l.
Exh: Agnew April 1968 (25)
Private collection
After the war Nash sometimes stayed at the Red
Lion at Whiteleaf, and worked in a group that in-
cluded his brother John and the wood engraver Eric
Daglish.

63   Towards Stone* 1921
Watercolour, chalk and pencil, 14 × 19¾ in.
s. & d. 1921 l.r.
Exh: LG 1924 (103); Tate 1948 (98)
*Whitworth Art Gallery, University of
Manchester*
Stone is the name of villages in Buckinghamshire
and Kent. A watercolour 'Stone Cliff' (15 × 21 in.
Coll: British Council) is dated July 1921 and is
recognisably Stone in Kent which has a chalk cliff
rising out of Romney Marsh, so this is probably also
in Kent.

64   Romney Marsh* *c.*1921
Watercolour, chalk and pencil, 15 × 23 in. s.l.r.
Exh: ?NEAC December 1921 (155), this title
Bernard Donoughue

65 Tench Pond in a Gale 1921–2
Watercolour, ink and pencil, $22\frac{3}{4} \times 15\frac{1}{2}$ in.
s. & d. 1921–2 l.r.
Exh: VB 1938 (17); Tate 1948 (93)
Tate Gallery, London
The picture was the first by Nash in the Tate's
permanent collection (1924).

66 Granary* 1922
Oil, $29\frac{1}{2} \times 24\frac{1}{2}$ in. s. & d. 1922 l.r.
Exh: OAC 1931 (24)
Lord Boyle of Handsworth

67 Wall Against the Sea 1922
Oil, 24×35 in. s. & d. 1922 l.r.
Exh: London Group October 1922 (69)
Victor D. Spark and James Graham and Sons
This was Nash's first picture shown at the Carnegie
International Exhibition in Pittsburgh (1923), and
it has remained in America ever since. Nash's first
submission to the Carnegie International in the pre-
vious year was the 1921 oil painting 'March Woods,
Whiteleaf' (Private collection), which was rejected
by the English jury.

68 Dymchurch, End of the Steps 1922
Watercolour and pencil, 15×22 in. s. & d.
1922 l.r.
Exh: Redfern 1937 (38)
Private collection

69 Night Tide* 1922
Watercolour and pencil, 15×22 in. s. & d.
1922 l.r.
Exh: Friday Club April 1922 (76); Tate
1948 (94)
Private collection

70 Promenade 1922
Watercolour, ink and pencil, 15×22 in.
s. & d. 1922 l.l.
Exh: NEAC June 1923 (172); Tate 1948 (95)
Arts Council of Great Britain

71 A Rainy Day 1922
Watercolour, chalk and pencil, $12\frac{1}{4} \times 19\frac{1}{2}$ in.
s. & d. 1922 l.r.
Exh: LG May 1945 (58a)
*National Art Gallery of New Zealand,
Wellington*

62

63

64

[63]

66

69

74

72 Places
Seven prints reproduced from woodblocks designed and engraved by Paul Nash with illustrations 'in prose'.
Heinemann, 1922
Private collection

73 The Chilterns 1923
Oil, 22 × 30 in. Unsigned
Exh: LG 1924 (107); Tate 1948 (6)
Miss Winifred Felce

74 The Sea* 1923
Oil, 22 × 35 in. s. & d. 1923 l.r.
Exh: LG 1924 (119)
Phillips Collection, Washington (Bequest of Miss Demarest)
The picture has been in America since it was sent to the Carnegie International Exhibition in 1929.

75 The Shore* 1923 (repr. on p.19)
Oil, 24 × 36 in. s. & d. 1923 l.r.
Exh: LG 1924 (121); Tate 1948 (7)
Leeds City Art Galleries

76 Chestnut Waters* 1923–37
Oil, 40 × 60 in. s.l.l.
Exh: LG 1924 (113)
National Gallery of Canada, Ottawa
The scene was at the home of Claude Lovat Fraser's parents at Buntingford, Hertfordshire, where Nash, who had been sharing a house with the Lovat Frasers at Dymchurch, went shortly after his friend's death in July 1921. In 1922 Nash made a wood engraving, 'Meeting Place, Buntingford', similar to this painting in design, but including a standing man and a recumbent woman (published in Nash's collection of landscape wood engravings *Places*, 1922; No.72).
Also in 1922 he made a watercolour 'Chestnut Waters' (s. & d. 1922, Desmond Coke sale, Sotheby's, 23 July 1931 (107), as 'Edge of the Lake') which has no figures and is very similar to this painting. Nash wrote to Coke (undated letter) when he was working on the oil asking for a photograph of the watercolour. Letters to Percy Withers (undated but *c.* November 1923) and Anthony Bertram (6 December 1923) show that Nash had started the oil that summer and was still unhappy with the result in December, but in a letter to Coke (undated but probably at the time of the Leicester Galleries exhibition in 1924) he wrote that it '*is* the best of

the lot and nearest to being an achievement I think'. At that time the picture was titled 'The Lake' and had a recumbent, nude female figure at the front, as in the 1922 wood engraving. The figure had been painted out by the time the picture was shown at the *Daily Express* Young Artists exhibition in 1927, but the title 'The Lake' was retained in several exhibitions before the picture was first shown as 'Chestnut Waters' at Tooth's in January 1938. Old photographs show that 'The Lake' was signed 'Paul Nash' and dated lower right, but the date (1924 ?) is illegible.

77 **The Canal Banks*** 1923
Watercolour and ink, 14¾ × 22 in. s. and inscribed with title l.r.
Exh: Redfern January 1949 (26)
Southampton Art Gallery

78 **Channel and Breakwater*** 1923
Watercolour, ink and chalk, 14¼ × 21¾ in.
s. & d. 1923 l.r.
Exh: Brook Street Gallery 1935
Harris Museum and Art Gallery, Preston

79 **Dymchurch Wall** 1923
Watercolour and pencil, 14½ × 21½ in. s. mid r.
Exh: Redfern 1942 (11); Tate 1948 (97)
Private collection

80 **Pond at Souldern** 1923
Chalk, 14½ × 20 in. s. & d. 1923 l.r.
Mrs Audrey Kennett
Part of a commission from Nash's friend Percy Withers of Souldern Court near Banbury for four watercolours of the house and village. In a letter of 15 May Nash said they were his first private commission (he had had public ones from the wartime Ministry of Information and the Canadian War Records), and he sent three, having abandoned the fourth. Withers subsequently acquired other watercolours from him. The view is from the window of the room Nash usually occupied when staying at Souldern. See also No.81.

81 **The Walnut Tree** 1923
Watercolour, chalk and pencil, 20 × 14½ in.
s. & d. 1923 l.r.
Mrs Audrey Kennett
The view is in the garden at Souldern Court; see No.80.

82 The Waterfall* 1923
Watercolour and ink, 10 × 14 in. s. & d. 1923 and
inscribed 'Rocky landscape' l.r.
Exh: LG 1927 (52)
Dr E. M. M. Besterman

Enlarged from a design made for the private edition
of T. E. Lawrence's *The Seven Pillars of Wisdom. A
Triumph* (1926) in which seven illustrations by Nash
are indexed though only five actually exist. This is
the last and probably the finest. Lawrence had first
contacted Nash when he acquired the oil painting
'Coast Scene' (1920) from the Rowley Gallery. In
August 1922 he asked Nash to join with other
artists in illustrating *The Seven Pillars of Wisdom*
from photographs, to which Nash agreed. Early in
January 1924, when Nash had delivered the illustrations, Lawrence wrote with enthusiasm about the
designs: 'The waterfall is magnificent', he said.

83 The Pond 1921–4
Oil, 30 × 25 in. s.l.r.
Exh: LG 1924 (106); Tate 1948 (4)
Private collection

Stylistically this is a work entirely of 1924, and the
earlier date which has always been associated with it
may refer not to the beginning of this picture but to
'Pond at Kimble' (Private collection) which is dated
1921 and is the watercolour from which this composition was taken. The oil is also known as 'Pond at
Iden', and comparison with many other pictures of
the pond which Nash made when he went to live
there in 1925 suggests that it may be of Iden.
Kimble is in Buckinghamshire not far from where
John Nash lived at Meadle.

84 Dymchurch Steps* 1924–44
Oil, 26 × 40 in. s. & d. 1924–44 l.r.
Exh: LG 1924 (120)
National Gallery of Canada, Ottawa

The picture was at Tooth's when it was bombed in
May 1941 and though there is no record that it was
damaged, Nash's reworking in 1944, which, his letters
show, included remodelling of the house and sky,
may have been connected with this. Up to 1944 it
was known as 'The Steps'.

84

85 Downs 1924
Watercolour on beige paper, $14\frac{1}{2} \times 20$ in.
s. & d. 1924 l.l.
Exh: LG 1924 (101)
City of Manchester Art Galleries

86 The Walnut Tree 1924
Chalk and pencil, $15\frac{1}{4} \times 21\frac{3}{4}$ in. s. & d. 1924 l.l.
City of Manchester Art Galleries
This walnut tree was at Bankshead, Brampton, Cumberland, the home of Ben and Winifred Nicholson, whom the Nashes visited in July 1924.

82

87 Genesis
Twelve woodcuts by Paul Nash with the first chapter of Genesis, Nonesuch Press 1924
Private collection

88 Rick Flat *c.*1925
Oil, 24×20 in. s.l.r.
Exh: Whitechapel 1929 (254)
Herbert Art Gallery, Coventry

89 The Colne* 1925
Watercolour and pencil, $15\frac{1}{2} \times 22\frac{3}{4}$ in. s. & d.
1925 l.r.
Exh: Mayor 1935 (8)
Mr and Mrs John Carter
Nash made several pictures of the River Colne when staying with his parents-in-law at Hillingdon, Middlesex. The reproduction of this one in E. Bernard Lintott's *The Art of Watercolour Painting* (1926) shows that it then had two figures of bathers just to the left of the bridge in an area that is now plain paper. The first owner was Desmond Coke, and Nash attended the Coke sale at Sotheby's, 23 July 1931, with John Carter who bought this picture (lot 107) while Nash bought 'Night Tide' (lot 133, No.69). The figures were probably removed then.

89

90 Design of Trees* 1925
Watercolour and pencil, 15×11 in. s. & d.
1925 l.l.
Exh: Mayor 1925 (4)
Trustees of the British Museum, London
Exhibited in 1932 by its first owner, the Contemporary Arts Society, as 'Spring Wood, Trees at Heston', which may be the location. The critic R. H. Wilenski lived at Heston, Middlesex, and Nash is recorded as staying there in 1924, but he probably went there at other times also.

90

91 **Dymchurch*** 1925
Watercolour and chalk, 20 × 30 in. s. & d. 1925
mid r.
Exh: ?NEAC April 1925 (177), this title
Trustees of the British Museum, London

92 **Boat Beached at Cagnes** 1925
Chalk, 5 × 8 in. Monogram
Private collection

93 **Boats on the Plage** 1925
Chalk, 5 × 8 in. Monogram l.r.
Exh: Warren 1927 (4)
Private collection

94 **Cros de Cagnes** 1925
Chalk, 5 × 8 in.
Private collection

95 Cros de Cagnes, Gates 1925
Chalk and pencil, $5\frac{1}{4} \times 8\frac{1}{4}$ in. Monogram
Private collection

96 Canterbury Bell 1926(?)
Oil, 29×19 in. Monogram l.r.
Exh: LAA 1927 (ex cat.); Tate 1948 (17)
Private collection

Nash wrote to Lance Sieveking about the picture, 19 November 1927: 'I am really glad if you like that picture and possess it. It is a queer painting and by no means everyone's. I had secretly hoped it would be bought by a friend who would know what was meant by it.' In fact it was bought in 1927 by Lady Juliet Duff, and Sieveking acquired it only in about 1944. Both Paul and Margaret Nash dated it 1926 while subsequently it has generally been dated 1927. Though the unusual subject perhaps points to 1927 when Nash was beginning to consciously extend his range, there seems insufficient reason to change the artist's date, especially as oil paintings earlier than 1928 are very difficult to attribute to a single year on stylistic grounds alone. A pencil study (22×17 in.)

belonged to Lance Sieveking (? gift of the artist when he failed to obtain the oil) and was in his sale at Christie's, 29 October 1971 (184), bt Hamet Gallery.

97 Mimosa Wood 1926
Oil, 20×26 in. s.l.r.
Exh: London Group June 1926 (46)
Art Gallery of New South Wales, Sydney
(Watson Bequest Fund)

The mimosa wood was outside the window of the Nashes' room at the Pension de la Plage, Cros de Cagnes, where they stayed in the early months of 1925.

98 Pond in the Fields* 1926(?)
Oil, 26×36 in. s.l.l.
Exh: LAA 1927 (ex cat.); Tate 1948 (19)
Private collection

Dated variously between 1925 and 1927; 1926 seems likely on grounds of style and was given under the first reproduction (*Paul Nash*, with an introduction by Anthony Bertram, Benn, 1927, plate 14).

91

98

101

99 Côte d'Azur 1926

Chalk, 11 × 17½ in. Monogram and d. 1926 l.r.
Exh: Redfern 1961 (78)
Norman Satinoff

Presumably begun or worked from a sketch done when the Nashes were at Cros de Cagnes in the early months of 1925.

100 St. Pancras Lilies 1927

Oil, 25 × 17½ in. Unsigned
Exh: LAA 1927 (ex cat.); Tate 1948 (16)
Ulster Museum, Belfast

This and another 1927 oil painting, 'St. Pancras' (coll: Cheltenham Art Gallery) seem to be the first Nash made from the window of his flat overlooking St. Pancras Station; see Nos.115 and 137.

101 Savernake* 1927

Oil, 30 × 20 in. Monogram l.l.
Exh: LAA 1927 (7); Tate 1948 (18)
R. D. Girouard

The view is of the Grand Avenue in Savernake Forest. Nash used to visit Savernake to stay with the Felce family whom he had met in the South of France in 1925; they later moved to Swanage and the Nashes borrowed their house there, Whitecliff Farm, from October 1934 to February 1935.

102 Still Life* 1927

Oil, 36 × 28 in. s. & inscribed with title on the back
Exh: LAA 1927 (53); Tate 1948 (12)
Leeds City Art Galleries

Included in the 1948 Tate catalogue as 'Bog Cotton', the title by which it has subsequently been known, but which was never used in Nash's lifetime.

103 Cactus* 1927–8

Oil, 20 × 16 in. Monogram l.l.
Exh: LG 1928 (71)
Borough of Harrogate Art Gallery

Margaret Nash listed the picture as 1927, a date which has generally been followed. But both the dry paint handling and the treatment of the subject, which is a view through a glass door at Oxenbridge Cottage, the Nashes' home at Iden, seems advanced for that date. Nash wrote to his wife in April 1928 that he had only four oil paintings ready for his big exhibition at the Leicester Galleries in November, and if this was one of them, he must have consciously abandoned experiment in the ones that followed to complete the necessary number of canvases quickly,

since many in the show were landscapes in his mode
of the mid-twenties.

104 Opening* 1927

Chalk and pencil, squared, 27¼ × 19 in.
Monogram and d. 1927 and inscribed 'Lance
and Natalie for thier [sic] union' l.l., and
'No 16 Abstract Design' on the back
Private collection

Used as a study for 'Opening' (No.121). It was given
by Nash to the Sievekings as a wedding present in
1929. Early photographs have Nash's monogram and
the date 1927 without the inscription, which shows
that, though the picture's abstraction is surprising as
early as 1927, it was not inaccurately predated when
the inscription was added in 1929.

105 Autumn Crocus* 1928

Oil, 39½ × 28 in. Monogram & d. 1928 l.r.
Exh: LG 1928 (67)
Mrs Constance J. W. Fettes

Paul and Margaret Nash both dated the picture
1927–8, though Paul wrote to Ruth Clark in June
1928 that he had 'started a new and rather exciting
picture', which Ruth Clark has confirmed was this
one. In subject and handling it is to some extent a
development of 'Cactus' (No.103) and was perhaps
also based on ideas he had been considering the
previous year. Up to 1934 the picture was known
as 'Interior'.

106 Diving Stage* 1928

Oil and pencil, 33 × 21 in. s.l.r.
Exh: LG 1928 (51)
British Council

The subject was at a swimming bath in a public park
at Caen where Nash was in June 1928; see also
No.118. It is quite common in his oils to see traces
of underdrawing on the canvas, but the extended use
of pencil in this experimental picture is probably
unique.

107 Tower* 1928

Oil, 28 × 20 in. Monogram l.r.
Exh: LG 1928 (70)
Mrs Hilda Colinvaux

A Cros de Cagnes subject dating from the 1925 visit,
the picture was titled 'Plage' when first reproduced
(*Studio*, November 1928), and has also been known
as 'Moorish Tower' and 'Moorish Tower, Cros de
Cagnes' since the 1930s. A virtually identical chalk
drawing (8¾ × 5¾ in. Private collection) was listed

102

104

103

by Nash in a set of pictures to be included in a show
of watercolours at the Leicester Galleries in November 1931, which in the event did not take place. It is
almost certainly a copy from the oil or from the
original sketch and not a preparatory work, and may
date from 1931.

[72]

105

107

106

109

108 Frozen Lake 1928
Watercolour, with faint squaring, 21 × 29½ in.
s. & d. 1928 l.l.
Exh: Redfern November 1936 (25); Tate 1948
(101)
Mrs Clare Neilson
The last of many versions Nash did of the lake at
Black Park, Iver Heath.

109 Blue House on the Shore* 1929(?)
Oil, 16½ × 28¾ in. s.l.l.
Exh: Tooth January 1932 (17) as 'The House
on the Shore'; Tate 1948 (15)
Tate Gallery, London
Margaret Nash listed the picture as *c.*1927 which
seems too early on account of the subject and tight
paint handling, and also raises the question why it
was not in the 1928 Leicester Galleries exhibition,
since it was not sold till 1939. The Nashes visited
Cros de Cagnes briefly in 1930 as well as staying
there in 1925, but nothing about this picture com-
pares closely with the ones that resulted from the
later trip. Other examples exist of subjects found in
1925 being completed only in 1929.

[73]

110 Coronilla 1929
   Oil, 24 × 20 in. Monogram l.r.
   Exh: VB 1932 (86)
   Private collection

The design relates to two wood engravings, 'Coronilla' of 1925 (Postan w64), which is almost identical, and 'Coronilla 2' (Postan w88) which has a standing male figure in the middle encircled by tendrils. The latter was first shown at the 11th annual exhibition of the Society of Woodengravers (Redfern Gallery, November 1930) and, though dated 1925–30 by Postan, may have been worked on only in 1930 and be a development away from abstraction after the oil painting, especially as it was not included in an early state in Nash's retrospective of wood engravings at the Redfern in July 1928.

Nash wrote 'The Flowering Room' on the back of a photograph of the oil, a title which appears nowhere else, but confirms what the subject of 'Coronilla 2' also suggests, that the design was inspired by Harold Monro's Symbolist poem 'Coronilla' (in his collection *Strange Meetings*, Poetry Bookshop, 1917), whose subject is the flower that is also the *femme fatale* who draws man into her room at night, drains his power without satisfying him, and kills him.

111 Dead Spring 1929
   Oil, 19½ × 15½ in. s. top l. and monogram l.r.
   Exh: LG July 1938 (128); Tate 1948 (27)
   Charles Kearley

Though apparently not exhibited till 1938, the picture was reproduced in *Studio*, December 1930, and in Joseph Duveen's *Twenty Years of British Art*, 1930.

112

112 February* 1929(?)
    Oil, 20 × 24 in. s.l.l.
    Exh: Tooth July 1930 (7)
    Vint Trust

The painting is difficult to date and the date is important because of its likely association with Nash's father's death in February 1929. Nash wrote '1930' on one photograph, and several bear the stamp of the Paul Guillaume-Brandon Davis Gallery, Nash's agents in 1929 and early 1930. If it was completed by November 1928 it would surely have been shown at the Leicester Galleries exhibition. But Ruth Clark has confirmed that Nash was considering the introduction of the tree stump, which was a radical stylistic departure, for some time before this, and Margaret Nash listed the picture as 1927. In technique, the picture is not specially advanced for 1929, but treatment such as that of the trees on the right exists in Nash's work through to 'Whiteleaf Cross' of 1931 (No.128).

113 Landscape at Iden* 1929 (repr. on p.19)
    Oil, $25\frac{3}{4} \times 27\frac{1}{2}$ in. s.l.l.
    Exh: Carnegie 1931 (261); Tate 1948 (24)
    Tate Gallery, London

Previously dated 1928 because it has been confused with the 1928 painting which originally had the same title but has been known since the 1948 Tate exhibition as 'The Pond, Iden' (Private collection). Newspaper reviews of Nash's November 1928 exhibition (in the Leicester Galleries press cuttings book) clearly show that the latter was the picture included (63) as 'Landscape at Iden', while the picture exhibited here is almost certainly the one included in Nash's 1929 list of oil paintings in Notebook 1 as 'Woodpile, fences etc. Iden', and mentioned in a letter to Margaret Nash of 25 July 1929, in which he wrote that he had 'greatly improved the woodstack landscape'. The view is from the back of Oxenbridge Cottage, Iden, where the Nashes lived from 1925 to 1930, to the Isle of Oxney in the distance. The exact dating is especially important since this picture is considerably more advanced in subject and handling than any of 1928.

114 Month of March* 1929
    Oil, 36 × 28 in. Monogram and s.l.r.
    Exh: VB 1932 (80); Tate 1948 (26)
    Private collection

Probably the picture listed in the 1929 list of oils in Notebook 1 as 'Orchard Iden March'. Before 1932 it was generally referred to simply as 'March'.

114

115

[75]

115 Northern Adventure* 1929
Oil, 36 × 28 in. s.l.l.
Exh: London Group October 1929 (155); Tate
1948 (30)
Aberdeen Art Gallery

The view, as in 'St. Pancras Lilies' (No.100), is through the window of the Nashes' fifth-floor flat, 176 Queen Alexandra Mansions, Judd Street, looking towards St. Pancras Station across the site of what is now Camden Town Hall but was then a vacant lot with an advertising hoarding. See also No.137.

116

116 Souvenir of Florence* 1929(?)
Oil, 26¾ × 17 in. Monogram l.r.
Exh: Carnegie 1929 (227)
Edward James Foundation

The subject was an urn in the restaurant of Florence railway station presumably drawn when the Nashes were there in March 1925. Diners (? the Nashes) are reflected in it. The picture appears in the list of 1929 oils in Notebook 1, but was dated 1928 in the catalogue of Nash's 1931 retrospective at the Oxford Arts Club; this is possible on grounds of style, but it was not shown in the 1928 Leicester Galleries exhibition. Margaret Nash's date of 1926 is too early for this subject in oil, though a sketch must have existed.

117 Lares* 1929–30
Oil, 24½ × 15½ in. Monogram l.r.
Exh: Leicester Art Gallery 1946 (32); Tate
1948 (29)
Private collection

The subject was the fireplace in the living room of the Nashes' London flat. The picture, which was also known by Nash as *Composition*, is in the 1929 list of oils in Notebook 1, but was dated 1930 on the back of a photograph. The later date is more in keeping with the subject and treatment. It was reproduced in *Studio*, December 1930.

117

118 Nest of the Siren* 1929–30 (repr. on p.20)
Oil, 30 × 20 in. s.l.l.
Exh: London Group October 1930 (176);
Tate 1948 (31)
Department of the Environment

Listed in Notebook 1 as a 1929 oil painting with the title 'Souvenir of Caen' and noted as 'scrapped'. It reappears, however, in the 1930 list both as 'Souvenir of Caen' and 'Siren', the titles bracketed so there is little doubt they refer to the same picture.

119

120

The wooden siren figure was seen by Nash when he was in Caen in June 1928; see No.106.

119 Interior * 1930
  Oil, 31¾ × 15½ in. s.l.r.
  Exh: Tooth 1931 (4)
  Private collection
Included in the 1930 list of oils in Notebook 1.

120 Wood on the Downs * 1930
  Oil, 28 × 36 in. s.l.l.
  Exh: Tooth July 1930 (5); Tate 1948 (28)
  Aberdeen Art Gallery
The subject is Ivinghoe Beacon in Buckinghamshire which Nash sometimes visited when staying with John Nash at Meadle. Describing this picture in a letter to Rex Nankivell of the Redfern Gallery, 22

December 1931, he remembered beginning it in March: 'The drawing for the painting was made there on the canvas and a separate drawing made with notes on the colours . . . . The sketch used to supplement the drawing was afterwards coloured and exhibited at Tooth's: Frank Rutter bought it ['Group of Beeches', exh: Tooth December 1930 (26), now coll: National Gallery of Victoria, Melbourne]. It differs slightly from the painting which was of course developed quite separately and unnaturalistically nearly a year later according to plan. The painting is simply a synthesis of a scene and mood of nature at a particular time of year – March. The red "foliage" is the effect of massed buds of beaches [sic] before they break.' In a letter to Hilda Felce in June 1930 Nash wrote: 'I am just finishing a large canvas of Ivinghoe Downs.'

121 Opening* 1930–31
   Oil, 32 × 20 in. s. & d. 1931 l.r.
   Exh: Tooth 1931 (5); Tate 1948 (35)
   Private collection

Titled when first shown 'Opening Abstract', but the shorter title was used by Nash for his 1943 Leeds retrospective. The picture is listed in Notebook 1 as 1930, and despite the date on the canvas is probably substantially of that year. Two drawings exist in connection with it, 'Opening' dated 1927 (No.104), which is more abstract than the oil, and 'Opening' dated 1930–1, squared and inscribed with the word MODERN in large but faint capitals lower right (12 × 8¼ in. Private collection). The inscription on the latter, which does not appear on the painting, connects with an inscription in Nash's hand on the back of a photograph of the oil: 'Bath House/Chermyeff [sic]/Modern Room.' Bath House was the home in Piccadilly of Lady Alice Ludlow, the first owner of the oil painting, but the meaning of the inscription is not clear since the architect and designer Serge Chermayeff was not then in England or a friend of Nash. It seems likely that Nash initially intended to paint an abstract picture with the word MODERN painted or stencilled on it in a Cubist manner. His change towards the more figurative rendering of the oil as it is could have been inspired by a comparable composition of the French Surrealist, Jean Lurçat, 'Environs de Delphe', shown at Lurçat's Lefevre Gallery exhibition in June 1930 and reproduced as a colour plate in *Apollo* in the same month.

121

127

122 Metamorphosis 1930–38
Oil, 25 × 30 in. s.l.l.
Exh: LG 1938 (42)
Art Gallery of South Australia, Adelaide
Though the picture has always been dated 1938 or
1937–8, the title is included in the 1930 list of oils in
Notebook 1, and the likeness of the subject to the
Toulon 'Voyages of the Moon' No.148 leaves no
doubt that this is the picture referred to. An undated
watercolour, 'Forest and Room' (8¼ × 9½ in. Coll:
Edward James Foundation), corresponds to the
composition of the oil except in minor details and in
lacking the nude figure on the left.

123 Glass Forest 1930
Watercolour and pencil, 12 × 8¾ in. Monogram
l.r.
Exh: Newcastle 1971 (17)
Edward James Foundation
Used as a study for 'Voyages of the Moon' (No.148).

124 Night Window 1930
Watercolour, chalk and pencil, 21 × 14 in.
s. & d. 1930 l.l.
Exh: Tooth December 1930 (37)
Private collection
Almost certainly done in the South of France, prob-
ably at Toulon.

125 Orford 1930
Watercolour and pencil, 15 × 21½ in.
s. & d. 1930 l.l.
Art Gallery of South Australia, Adelaide
A very similar picture, but without a sailing boat in
the right foreground, was shown at Tooth's in
December 1930 (25). The subject is Orford, Suffolk,
where Nash went when staying with Lance Sieveking
at Snape in September 1930. It is one of Nash's
earliest pictures to have been developed from a
photograph (see *Paul Nash's Photographs*, plate 1).

PAUL NASH AND EDWARD BURRA
126 Rough on Rats *c.*1930
Pencil and collage, 19¼ × 14½ in.
Private collection

127 Kinetic Feature* 1931
Oil, 26 × 20 in. s. & d. 1931 l.r. and, more
obscurely, s.l.l.
Exh: Tooth 1931 (2); Tate 1948 (34)
Tate Gallery, London

128 Whiteleaf Cross 1931
Oil, 21 × 30 in. Monogram l.r.
Exh: Carnegie 1931 (260); Tate 1948 (36)
Estate of W. W. Wadsworth
Previously dated 1932, while the picture shown at
the 1931 Carnegie International was thought to have
been the 1920 painting of this title (20 × 24 in. Coll:
National Gallery of South Africa, Capetown). Nash
never sent an eleven-year-old picture to the Carnegie
International, and in 1931, when he was himself the
English member of the jury, he would have been
most likely to have sent a new one. No.59 is another
view of the subject.

129 Harbour and Room* 1932–6
Oil, 36 × 28 in. s.l.l.
Exh: ISE 1936 (240)
Edward James Foundation
The design, like those of 'Voyages of the Moon'
(No.148) and 'Metamorphosis' (No.122), originated
at Toulon in February 1930. The picture has been
ascribed to various dates between 1929 and 1936.
Nash dated it 1932–6, and the first time it was reproduced, in Herbert Read's *Surrealism* (1936) it was
given to 1936. Nash's earlier date suggests it was
started after the completion of the near-identical
watercolour of the same title (20¼ × 15½ in. Private
collection) which is dated 1931, and his second date
indicates that it may have been left unfinished and
completed to coincide with the International Surrealist Exhibition. A study for part of the right-hand
side (6¾ × 9¾ in. Coll: Fine Art Society) is inscribed
'Study at Toulon no 6' and dated 1930, and also
bears an inscribed note about mounting which includes a reference to 'no 3'. Other studies connected
with the scene exist (e.g. of boats in the harbour),
but none directly connected with the composition,
so the identity of the other numbers is unknown.

130 Atlantic 1932
Watercolour, chalk and pencil, 22 × 15¼ in.
s. & d. 1932 l.r.
Exh: LG 1932 (12)
Lord Croft
From a set of watercolours including Nos.132, 136
and 138 of aspects of the ships on which Nash travelled to and from America in September and October
1931. With the probable exception of 136 they all
relate to photographs.

129

131 Group for a Sculptor 1932
Watercolour and pencil, 15½ × 23 in. s. twice l.l.
and l r.
Exh: LG 1932 (20); Tate 1948 (104)
Henry Moore

132 Liner 1932
Watercolour, chalk and pencil, 15 × 22 in.
s. & d. 1932 l.l.
Exh: LG 1932 (20)
Private collection
See No.130.

133 March Woods 1932
Watercolour and pencil, 15 × 22 in. s.l.l.
Exh: LG 1932 (25)
Mrs Enid Levetus

134 Monuments 1932
Watercolour and pencil, 22 × 15 in. Unsigned
Exh: LG 1932 (6)
Private collection
The subject is the stone busts outside the Sheldonian Theatre, Oxford. Nash lectured at the Oxford Arts Club on 18 May 1932 and wrote to Lillah Macarthy (12 May) asking to be accommodated. 'I am anxious to do a few drawings in Oxford,' he said. Nash also made a close-up view of one of the heads, 'Souvenir of Oxford' (22 × 12¾ in. Private collection).

135 River 1932
Watercolour and pencil, 15½ × 22¼ in. s.l.r.
Exh: LG 1932 (3)
Miss Barbara Nash
The river is the Rother at Rye. The picture is also known as 'Swings'.

136 Ship Interior 1932
Watercolour and pencil, 21½ × 14¾ in. s. & d. 1932 l.r.
Exh: LG 1932 (15)
Anthony Bertram
Also known as 'Sundeck, S.S. Mauretania', the boat on which Nash sailed to America. See No.130.

137 Skeleton* 1932
Watercolour, 22 × 15 in. s. & d. 1932 l.r.
Exh: LG 1932 (38)
Musée National d'Art Moderne, Paris
The view is from the Nashes' flat in Queen Alexandra Mansions towards St. Pancras Station similar to that in 'Northern Adventure' (No.115), except that a fairground switchback has replaced the advertising hoardings. It was described by Conrad Aiken in his autobiography *Ushant*, 1963 (p.234): 'In the vacant lot between Paul's flat and St. Pancras was a newly-arrived fair with roundabouts and swings, and the liquid squeal of a Calliope; but more importantly . . . [there was] a switch-back, a genuine nerve-shattering Coney Island roller-coaster.' Ratebooks in the archive of the present London borough of Camden show that the site was used as an amusement park in 1931 (information from W. R. Maidment, director of Libraries and Arts), which presumably dates the origin of the picture. Nash made another, horizontal,

version, 'St Pancras Landscape' (13¼ × 20 in. Private collection).

138 Voyage* 1932
Watercolour, 15¾ × 22½ in. s.l.r.
Exh: LG 1932 (10)
Wadsworth Atheneum, Hartford (Ella Gallup Sumner and Mary Catlin Sumner Collection)
See No.130.

139 Urne Buriall and The Garden of Cyrus
by Sir Thomas Browne, edited by John Carter, with 30 drawings by Paul Nash, Cassell 1932.
A. W. Harris
The book, a new edition of Browne's twin treatises originally published separately in 1658, was planned by John Carter with Desmond Flower of Cassell and Nash in 1930, and an agreement was made in April 1931 with Oliver Simon of the Curwen Press to produce the book, the plates to be made from monochrome collotypes coloured by hand in watercolour over stencils by the staff of the Curwen Press. Nash made the drawings between summer 1931 and spring 1932. The four watercolours exhibited here (Nos.140–43) are from a total of five watercolours and three oils enlarged in 1932 and 1933 from a set of small watercolours which were probably used to guide the Curwen artists and for Nash to check their work.

140 Mansions of the Dead 1932
Watercolour and pencil, 22 × 15 in. s.l.r.
Exh: LG 1932 (40)
Edward James Foundation
See No.139.

141 The Order of Five 1932
Watercolour, ink, chalk and pencil, 22 × 15 in. s.l.r.
Exh: LG 1932 (39)
Private collection
See No.139.

142 Poised Objects 1932
Watercolour, chalk and pencil, 22 × 15 in. s.l.r.
Exh: LG 1932 (21) as 'Composition'; Tate 1948 (105)
Junior Common Room, St Anne's College, Oxford
Previously dated 1933 except in the 1948 Tate catalogue; a reproduction titled *Composition* in the *Architectural Review*, October 1932, accompanying an article by Anthony Bertram on the 1932 Leicester

137

Galleries exhibition, confirms that this was the picture shown there as *Composition* – the title under which it was also shown at Unit One. See No.139.

143 Quincunx 1932
Watercolour, ink and chalk, 21 × 14 in. s.l.l.
Exh: LG 1932 (29); Tate 1948 (107)
Private collection
See No.139.

144 Event on the Downs* 1934(?)
Oil, 20 × 24 in. s.l.l.
Exh: AIA 1937 (188); Tate 1948 (37)
Department of the Environment
The view is from Whitecliff Farm, Swanage, over Ballard Down to the sea. It is generally dated 1934, when Nash stayed at Whitecliff from October to the following February, but 1933 in the 1948 Tate catalogue, which is a possible date as Nash visited Whitecliff in 1933, though it raises the question why the picture was not shown at Unit One (April 1934).

138

144

145 Landscape of the Megaliths* 1934

Oil, $19\frac{5}{8} \times 28\frac{3}{4}$ in. s.l.l.

Exh: Unit One 1934 (9) as 'Landscape
Composition', but not on tour; Tate 1948 (39)

British Council

Margaret Nash said this was Paul's first painting of
the Avebury stones, which he saw in August 1933.
Nash himself gave the following description of
Avebury in 'Picture History':

145

> The preoccupation of the stones has always been a
> separate pursuit and interest aside from that of
> object-personages. My interest began with the
> discovery of the Avebury megaliths when I was
> staying at Marlborough in the Summer of 1933.
> The great stones were then in their wild state, so
> to speak. Some were half covered by the grass,
> others stood up in the cornfields were entangled

and overgrown in the copses, some were buried under the turf. But they were always wonderful and disquieting, and, as I saw them then, I shall always remember them. . . .

Their colouring and pattern, their patina of golden lichen, all enhanced their strange forms and mystical significance. Thereafter, I hunted stones, by the seashore, on the downs, in the furrows.

In most instances, the pictures coming out of this preoccupation were concerned with stones seen solely as objects in relation to landscape, as in the 'Landscape of the Megaliths' series, or as stone objects related to other objects, or groups of of objects. But later certain stone personages evolved, such as the stone birds in the 'Nest of Wild Stones' and the more 'abstract' forms in 'Encounter in the Afternoon'. In the later, larger compositions – 'Circle of the Monoliths' and 'Nocturnal Landscape' the stones have a character influenced by the conditions of Dream.

An inscription in Nash's hand on the back of a photograph shows that the first title was 'Landscape Composition' and that it was shown at Unit One. Nash wrote about his feelings towards abstraction and landscape in a letter to Bertram dated 14 April 1934.

I feel I am beginning now to find my way between the claims of 'Abstractions' and pure interpretation. As you know, I am far too interested in the character of landscape and natural forms generally – from a pictorial point of view – ever to abandon painting *after* Nature of some kind or other. But I want a wider aspect, a different angle of vision as it were. This I am beginning to find through symbolism and in the power of association – not the rather freakish unlikely association of objects, so much as the *right* association as I feel it to be . . . I desire to penetrate further – or if you like fling my net wider to include a relationship of spiritual personality – only I suppose I must find another word for spiritual, or be misunderstood. I confess I have not reached a very articulate stage, but perhaps you see my drift.

146 Stone Tree* 1934
Oil, 23 × 16 in. s.l.r.
Exh: Unit One 1934 (13), but not on tour
Private collection

Generally misdated 1938 since the Unit One show. The subject seems to have been a fossilised tree, since Nash wrote to Winifred Felce, 7 April 1934,

with reference to the Unit One show: 'Stone Tree also derived from the stone we found at the White-cliff farm.'

147 View Ƨ 1934
Oil, 23 × 16 in. Monogram l.r.
Exh: Tooth December 1938 (9)
Bradford Metropolitan Council, Art Galleries and Museums

The picture is one of a pair (with 'View Я'), the design of which were inspired by the view from the room of the Hôtel des Princes, Nice, where the Nashes stayed in the early months of 1934. The letters were part of the name of the hotel attached to the first-floor balconies, which Nash painted in reverse because he saw them from the back. Nash explained the work as follows:

. . . Then I began to like the letters individually as pieces of ornament in relation to the scene beyond. But I did not like them *where they were*. It was obvious that if I painted the word or words as these on the balcony with the sea in the distance I should not be able to make either a good combination of the two opposing elements or give the true ornamental or formal value which the letters seemed to me to possess in themselves. . . . The problem was solved by detaching the letters I wanted and setting them in a different relationship, when they were on equal terms, so to say, with the rest of the pictorial matter. . . . Now it seemed to me I had what I wanted – Actually I had rather more than I first thought of because in the act of imagination necessary to make this state of things, I wanted a certain new dramatic interest and a certain mystery in the meaning of each picture.

Nash took photographs of the letters (see *Paul Nash's Photographs*, plate 14), and it is likely, since the pictures were not shown at Unit One in April, that they were done, or at least finished, in England from photographs. 'View Ƨ' was first reproduced in *Apollo*, April 1935, as 'Souvenir of Nice' (the title of a watercolour and never properly belonging to this picture).

148 Voyages of the Moon* 1934–7
Oil, 28 × 21¼ in. Monogram and s. & d. 1934 l.r.
Exh: Unit One 1934 (23) and tour 1934–5 (40);
Tate 1948 (44)
Tate Gallery, London

The design was based on the dining room of the Hôtel du Port et des Négociants, Toulon, where the

Nashes stayed in February 1930 (see also Nos.122 and 129). The room had globe lights and tall mirrors on facing walls which gave the illusion of endless recession. Nash recorded the design in the watercolour 'Glass Forest' (No.123) which, apart from the moon, corresponds closely to this oil as it was in 1934 when titled 'Formal Dream'. The reintroduction of the moon was one of several changes, including modifications around the area of the door on the right, made in 1937 when the picture was brought to its present state and title.

146

149 Wood Fetish 1934

Watercolour and pencil, 22 × 14½ in. s. mid. l.
Exh: Redfern 1935 (35)
Commander Michael Watson R.N.

A drawing of Nash's first 'found object', 'Marsh Personage' (see *Paul Nash's Photographs*, plate 36), which was two pieces of driftwood he found in the valley of the Rother when staying at Small Hythe in Kent in August 1934, and which was itself exhibited at the International Surrealist Exhibition in June 1936. See No.160.

150 Landscape of the Megaliths 1934–7(?)

Watercolour and chalk, 19¾ × 29¾ in. s.l.l.
Exh: Redfern 1937 (26); Tate 1948 (112)
Albright-Knox Art Gallery, Buffalo (Room of Contemporary Art Fund)

Since the catalogue of the 1937 Redfern exhibition the picture has always been dated 1937, but a virtually identical colour lithograph, published by Contemporary Lithographs Ltd, was reproduced in the *Architectural Review* in January 1937, so at least the design must have existed earlier. Margaret Nash wrote in her 'Memoir' (p.76) that 'the well known watercolour Landscape of the Megaliths' was painted early in 1934; this could be taken as a confusion with the oil of the same title (see No.145), which was certainly painted early in 1934, if it were not for the coincidence that Nash's contribution to the *Unit One* volume (published April 1934) contains verbal imagery very close to the watercolour:

148

> Last summer, I walked in a field near Avebury where two rough monoliths stand up, sixteen feet high, miraculously patterned with black and orange lichen, remnants of the avenue of stones which led to the Great Circle. A mile away, a green pyramid casts a gigantic shadow. In the hedge, at hand, the white trumpet of a convolvulus turns from its spiral stem, following the sun. In my art I would solve such an equation.

151

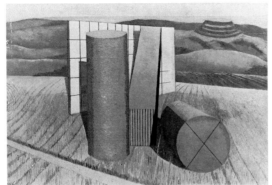

151 Equivalents for the Megaliths* 1935
  Oil, 18 × 26 in. s.l.l.
  Exh: VB 1938 (12); Tate 1948 (40)
  Tate Gallery, London

In a letter to Lance Sieveking of 4 May 1937 Nash wrote:

> These groups are impressive as forms opposed to their surroundings, both by virtue of their actual composition of lines and masses and planes, directions and volumes; and in the irrational sense, their suggestion of a super-reality. They are dramatic, also, however, as symbols of their antiquity, as hallowed remnants of an almost unknown civilization. In designing the picture I wished to avoid the very powerful influence of this antiquarian suggestion, and to insist only upon the dramatic qualities of a composition of shapes equivalent to the prone or upright stones simply as upright or prone, or leaning masses, grouped together in a scene of open fields and hills. Beyond that resolve the picture cannot be traced, logically. It developed inevitably in its own way.

152

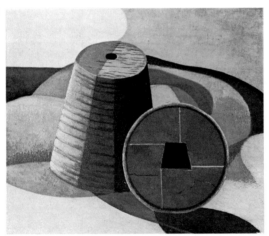

152 Mineral Objects* 1935
  Oil, 20 × 24 in. Monogram mid. r.
  Exh: AIA 1935 as 'Rotary Composition'
  Governor and Company of the Bank of England

The mineral objects are Kimmeridge 'coal money', which Nash saw in the Dorchester Museum and described in his *Dorset Shell Guide*, pp.16–17. Made of shale from the Kimmeridge coast area of Dorset, the objects were at one time thought to have been used as money but they are in fact throw-outs from lathes. The picture was known as 'Rotary Composition' till it was shown under its present title at the Leicester Galleries in 1938. Nash also wrote 'Apotheosis of the Shale' on the back of a photograph.

153 Objects in Relation* 1935 (repr. on p.20)
  Oil, 20 × 24 in. s.l.l.
  Exh: Lefevre Gallery March 1936 (26); Tate 1948 (41)
  St. Paul's School, London

The design follows closely that of a small tempera painting, 'Composition' (5 × 6 in.), exhibited in a mixed show at the 34 Gallery, April 1934 (19).

154 Empty Room 1935(?)
  Watercolour and pencil, 15 × 22 in. Unsigned
  Exh: Agnew February 1936 (91); Tate 1948 (113)
  Private collection

Since the 1937 Redfern exhibition the picture has been dated 1937, but the Agnew exhibition makes this impossible. The empty room from which the idea for the picture was taken was on the top floor of the house overlooking the sea at Swanage which belonged to Archibald Russell, an amateur lepidopterist who inveigled moths into the room at night by leaving the window open and a strong light burning.

155 Sea Wall 1935
   Watercolour and pencil, 15 × 22 in. s.l.l.
   Exh: Redfern 1935 (23)
   C. L. Brook
Often known as 'Sea Wall, Swanage', but actually based on the Cobb, the small walled harbour at Lyme Regis, of which several photographs by Nash exist.

156 The Voyage of the Fungus 1935–6
   Watercolour and chalk, 11¼ × 15½ in. s.l.l.
   Exh: Redfern April 1936 (30)
   Edward James Foundation
The location is Swanage Bay. The funguses were taken from a photograph (see *Paul Nash's Photographs*, plate 30).

157 Encounter in the Afternoon 1936
   Oil, 20 × 30 in. s.l.l.
   Exh: ISE 1936 (241)
   Edward James Foundation
Nash wrote of his discovery of the flints used in this picture in 'The Nest of the Wild Stones' (in *The Painter's Object*, ed. Myfanwy Evans, 1937): 'Sometimes one may find a pair of stone birds almost side by side. Inseparable complements, in true relation. Yet, lying there in the grass never finding each other until I found them that afternoon on the Sussex Downs, during an attempt to remember whether Edward James lived at East or West Dean. That problem was not then solved, but so soon as my stones came into my hands their equation was solved and they were united for ever. And directly Edward James saw the picture of these two, he wished to acquire it.' The watercolour study (7½ × 11 in. squared) was given by Nash to Herbert Read.

158 Environment for Two Objects 1936
   Oil, 20½ × 30½ in. s.l.l.
   Exh: Rosenberg & Helft January 1937 (14);
   Tate 1948 (43)
   Beaverbrook Art Gallery, Fredericton, New Brunswick, Canada

Previously dated 1937, but the date of the Rosenberg & Helft exhibition, in which this replaced 'Landscape from a Dream' (No.159) at the last moment, makes 1937 almost impossible. The porcelain doll's head also appears in 'Changing Scene' (No.162). The charred wooden door handle was used in one of his Surrealist objects, 'Burnt Offering' (c.1936–7).

159 Landscape from a Dream* 1936–8
   (repr. on p.29)
   Oil, 26½ × 40 in. s.l.l.
   Exh: LG 1938 (40); Tate 1948 (49)
   Tate Gallery, London
Always dated 1938 until it was pointed out in the Tate Gallery catalogue (*Modern British Paintings*, Vol.2, 1964) that it was planned for inclusion in a mixed exhibition at Rosenberg & Helft, January 1937 (14), with a note that it was unfinished because of Nash's illness and replaced by 'Environment for Two Objects' (No.158). A near identical watercolour (15 × 22 in. squared. Private collection) was shown at Nash's 1937 Redfern Gallery exhibition of watercolours, and was dated 1937 in the catalogue; but 1936 seems a more likely date for the watercolour since the squaring suggests it was preparatory for the oil. The hawk in the picture was painted from an Egyptian carving now on the artist's tomb, and the spheres were derived from balls of prairie grass Nash had seen in a film.

160 Swanage *c.*1936
   Collaged photographs, watercolour and pencil, 13¼ × 16½ in. Monogram and inscr. with title l.r.
   Exh: Hamet 1973 (46)
   Tate Gallery, London
The images are explained in full in *The Tate Gallery 1972–4*, 1975, pp.204–11. The third object from the right is 'Marsh Personage'; see No.149.

161 The Landscape at Penn Pits* 1937
   (repr. on p.29)
   Watercolour, 16 × 23 in. s.l.l.
   Exh: Mayor November 1937 (5)
   Victoria and Albert Museum, London
Ascribed to various dates, but this one is likely on grounds of style, and appeared under the first reproduction, in *Signature*, July 1938.

162 Changing Scene 1937
   Oil, 26 × 21 in. s.l.l.
   Exh: LG 1938 (41)
   Private collection

The view is from Whitecliff Farm, Swanage, to Ballard Down. The head was painted from the porcelain doll also used in 'Environment for Two Objects' (No.158). Nash was seen holding it in a photograph reproduced in the *Manchester Evening News*, 12 February 1937, illustrating his article 'Personal View'.

163 Circle of the Monoliths 1937–8
Oil, 31 × 41 in. s. mid l.
Exh: LG 1938 (37); Tate 1948 (45)
Leeds City Art Galleries
Always previously dated 1938 except in the Tate 1948 catalogue where it is ascribed to 1937–8; the latter is borne out by a pencil and watercolour sketch given by the artist to John and Myfanwy Piper and inscribed 'Christmas 1937'. Nash gave a description of the work in 'Picture History':

'Circle of the Monoliths' is a picture of the kind of dream that might come to a sleeper who had lately spent hours on the shore of Swanage Bay where the cliffs are like these cliffs. And not long before the dreamer had walked in a field near Avebury and wondered at the strangely patterned megaliths that stood up here and there between the hedges. Perhaps each place made a very deep impression, deeper than he knew. But in the dream, the sea invades the fields, the hedges take the place of breakwaters, the great monoliths and their pools of shadow seem to reappear in the form of needles of white chalk, another kind of monolith. And to complete the magic circle, a spout of water arises from the sea in a narrow cone.

I do not say I dreamed the picture. It is simply a painting concerned with two landscapes or a landscape and a seascape of particular character and peculiar beauty with whose appearance I was intimate, even enchanted. The paralogism of dream frees me to paint a picture where the two images are fused.

164 Stone Forest 1937
Watercolour, chalk and pencil, 23⅛ × 15¼ in. s.l.r.
Exh: Redfern 1937 (15)
Whitworth Art Gallery, University of Manchester
The design was based on a postcard Nash had of the Fossil Forest at Lulworth, Dorset.

165 Sunset at Worth Matravers 1937
Watercolour and chalk, 7 × 10 in. Unsigned
Exh: Redfern 1937 (27); Tate 1948 (118)
Private collection

166 Three Rooms 1937
Watercolour and pencil, 15½ × 11¼ in. Unsigned
Exh: Redfern 1937 (46)
Edward James Foundation
The basic structure of this unusual design was derived from a plate in *The Practice of Perspective . . . by a Jesuit of Paris* [Abbé Dubreuil], Paris, 1726, p.133, of which Nash owned a copy.

167 Wood of the Nightmares' Tales* 1937
Watercolour and chalk, 10 × 7 in. Monogram l.l.
Exh: Redfern 1937 (41); Tate 1948 (114)
Richard Smart

168 Wood Sea 1937
Watercolour and pencil, 15¾ × 22¾ in. s.l.l.
Exh: Redfern 1937 (18); Tate 1948 (117)
Lord Boyle of Handsworth

169 Forest *c*.1937
Wood, 12 × 12 in.
Exh: London Gallery 1937 (17) in the category 'Surrealist object'
Sir Roland Penrose
The trees are wooden glove-stretchers and are interchangeable between the slots in the support. They appear in the photograph of Nash in his studio reproduced in *Poet and Painter*, plate 15, and were also the model for the trees in the 1937 watercolour 'Wood on the Hill'.

170 Made Objects

a Only Egg *c*.1937
Two flints, a piece of shale and photomontage in a glass-fronted wooden box, 12 × 6 × 6 in.
Exh: London Gallery 1937 (72) in the category 'object collage'
Mrs Clare Neilson
The two flints resemble a bird guarding her egg, the upright one being similar to (but not identical with) the upright flint in 'Encounter in the Afternoon' (No.157). The montage is made up of two photographs, one showing the shore at Kimmeridge, Dorset, the other of the concrete trough used in the 1936 watercolour 'Object in the Fields' (22 × 12½ in., ex coll: James Thurber).

b–i Photographs of assemblages made by Nash and no longer extant. The categories are Nash's.

b The Archer 1936(?)
   Wood, glass and seaweed
   Category: Interpreted object
   Exh: LG 1938 (48)

The wooden object was the hull section of a small toy boat and seems to represent the archer and/or the bow, while the glass tube is presumably the arrow. 'The Archer' was reproduced in Herbert Read's *Surrealism* (1936). It appears in two oil paintings, 'The Archer' (28 × 36 in. Coll: Southampton Art Gallery) and 'The Archer Overthrown' (28 × 36 in. Private collection), which Nash said were begun in 1930 and 1931 respectively, though they were both first exhibited at the Artists' International Association in 1937. If the paintings were close to their present state in 1930–31, the object must have already been made, and would be by far the earliest of Nash's made objects: it seems likelier, though, that the first versions of the oils were landscapes without the archer who was added after 1936.

Nash wrote a note on the subject for an editor at Penguin Books who had a query from a reader of the Penguin Modern Painters book on Nash (1944), in which the oil painting 'The Archer' was reproduced: 'The Archer portrays an incident in a purely private fairy tale which originated with the object The Archer. Two or three characters generally appear, the Archer, the Shadow and the Wheel.' In his biography of the artist Anthony Bertram suggested, probably rightly, that the archer was Apollo and the wheel that was his target in the oil painting was a sunwheel.

PAUL AND MARGARET NASH
c Basket for Found Objects 1936–7
   Category: Object for everyday use
   Exh: London Gallery 1937 (82)

d Burnt Offering 1936–7
   Charred wooden door handle with an old iron lock on stone
   Category: Perturbed object or Perturbed object assembled
   Exh: London Gallery 1937 (93)

The handle appears in the oil painting 'Environment for Two Objects' (No.158).

e Encounter of the Wild Horns 1937
   Horn, wood and stone, 7 × 8 × 4 in.
   Exh: Redfern 1937 (53) as a work of 1937

The horn (No.238b) appears in three pictures: 'Landscape of Bleached Objects' (1934, oil, 15 × 20 in. Destroyed in the war), 'Ballard Phantom' (1935, watercolour, 16 × 23 in. Private collection) and 'Nocturnal Landscape' (No.171).

f   Moon Aviary 1936–7
Wood, stone and ivory bobbins
Category: Constructed object
Exh: London Gallery 1937 (101)

A piece of blue glass was supplied at the London Gallery to view the object through, and a notice was attached to the exhibit: 'Please use the mask when looking at the aviary'. A related piece also shown at the London Gallery (16) was 'Homes without Hands', in which two ivory bobbins, representing birds, were mounted on the cedarwood box compartments used in 'Mansions of the Dead' (No.140). 'Homes without Hands' was dedicated to Giacometti and somewhat resembles his 'The Palace at 4 a.m.' which was in the 1936 International Surrealist Exhibition.

g   Sea Scraper 1936(?)
Cork, seaweed and ivory on wooden base
Exh: ISE 1936 (250) as 'Found Object
Interpreted (Seaweed and Cork)'

A very similar object was painted in the watercolour 'Object on the Sands', 1935 (coll: Edward James Foundation).

h   Victorian Paradox 1937
Wood, ivory hand and ivory bobbin on wooden base, $8\frac{3}{4} \times 6\frac{1}{2} \times 4\frac{1}{4}$ in.
Exh: Redfern 1937 (54) as a work of 1937

Sometimes shown under a glass dome.

i   Nest of the Wild Stones 1936–7
Four flints
Category: Found Object Interpreted
Exh: London Gallery 1937 (58)

The object and the related watercolour of the same title (15 × 22 in. coll: Arts Council) were illustrations to Nash's article also called 'The Nest of the Wild Stones' in *The Painter's Object*, 1937.

171 **Nocturnal Landscape** 1938
Oil, 30 × $40\frac{1}{2}$ in. s.l.l.
Exh: LG 1938 (43); Tate 1948 (48)
City of Manchester Art Galleries

A watercolour and ink sketch ($7\frac{1}{2} \times 9\frac{1}{2}$ in.) for, or after, the painting was shown in a mixed exhibition of English art at the Galleria d'Arte Sant'Ambrogio, Milan, October 1973 (9).

172 **Nostalgic Landscape** 1922–38
Oil, 28 × 20 in. s.l.l.
Exh: LG 1938 (31); Tate 1948 (8)
Leicester Museums and Art Galleries

The subject is a sluice building at the Hythe end of the Dymchurch wall, the appearance of which has since been modified by the addition of a brick-built lookout post on the top during the second world war. Nash started the picture when living at Dymchurch, and dated it 1923–38 in the Penguin Modern Painters book on his work (ed. Herbert Read, 1944); but the squared study (7 × 5 in. Coll: Hamet Fine Art) is dated 1922, and it seems likely that Nash misremembered the earlier date. The handling of the tower in the painting differs from the study in the introduction of the interior tunnel effect and the formation of the upper roundel into an equivalent for the sun. The colour and paint application show that the oil is almost entirely a work of 1938.

173 **Image of the Stag** 1938
Watercolour and chalk, $11\frac{1}{8} \times 15\frac{1}{2}$ in. s.l.l.
Exh: Tooth July 1939 (8); Tate 1948 (119)
Lord Clark

174 **Landscape of the Death Watch** 1938
Watercolour and chalk, 11 × $15\frac{1}{2}$ in. s.l.l.
Exh: Tooth December 1938 (13); Tate 1948 (120)
Lord Croft

175 **Silbury Hill** c.1938
Watercolour and pencil, $15\frac{1}{4} \times 22\frac{1}{4}$ in. s.l.r.
Exh: Newcastle 1971 (34)
H. Riley

176 **Clifton, the Bridge** 1939
Watercolour and pencil, 11 × 15 in. s.l.l.
Mr and Mrs John Carter

One of several views of Clifton Suspension Bridge from the Clifton Spa Hotel which Nash made when he visited Bristol in March 1939, and collected material for his article about the bridge, 'The Giant's Stride' (*Architectural Review*, September 1939). It has previously been mistakenly known as 'To the Memory of Brunel' in confusion with another watercolour of the same view ($10\frac{3}{4} \times 14\frac{3}{4}$ in. Coll: British Council). See No.180.

177 Monster Field* 1939
  Oil, 30 × 40 in. s.l.l.
  Exh: Tooth July 1939 (11)
  Durban Art Gallery, South Africa

Monster Field was Nash's name for a field on Carswalls Farm near Newent, Gloucestershire, which he discovered from Madams. He found an animal quality in the skeletons of dead elms which he photographed. From the photographs he made two watercolours, 'Monster, study 1' (No.179) and 'Monster, study 2'. Nash also wrote a descriptive and imaginative essay 'Monster Field', dated London 1939, for publication with five photographs, the oil and two watercolours, in the Surrealist art periodical *London Bulletin*; this, however, ceased publication with the coming of the war. The essay was published in the *Architectural Review*, September 1939, but with only two photographs and none of the pictures as illustrations; it was reissued as a booklet with a complete set of illustrations by Counterpoint Publications, Oxford, 1946.

Nash wrote to Clare Neilson, who had been with him when he discovered Monster Field, 16 May 1939: 'I am working away at Monster Field, it should be finished this week. I am planning to exhibit it at Tooth's with its accompanying colour studies, and like drawings.' The oil and two watercolours were shown at Tooth's in July. The photographs were evidently taken in summer, and therefore probably on Nash's first visit to Madams in June–July 1938. Documentary evidence suggests here, as with 'Wood on the Downs' (No.120), that nearly a year elapsed before Nash worked on a landscape idea in oil. But even this is less than the four years (1925–9) which elapsed before some of the Cros de Cagnes pictures were completed.

177

178 Monster Shore 1939
  Oil, 28 × 36 in. s.l.l.
  Exh: Lefevre Gallery January 1940 (37)
  Hamilton Art Gallery, Hamilton, Ontario

The design relates to two 1938 watercolours, 'The Severn' (11 × 16 in. Private collection), which is a representational riverscape, and 'The Seven Bore near Pimlico Sands' (11 × 15 in. Private collection), which has added Surrealist elements like the oil. It is not known whether Nash ever saw the Severn Bore, but as an apparently unaccountable natural force it would certainly have interested him, and the sinister inventions in the oil can be regarded as an elaboration of its implications.

The painting has been dated 1939 except by Nash who dated a photograph 1939–41, and wrote in 'Picture History' that 'just previous to my appointment to the Air Ministry [March 1940] I carried out and completed the canvas I had begun before the war, a sequel to Monster Field which was called Monster Shore'. In view of the Lefevre Gallery exhibition the picture must have been finished by the end of 1939.

179 Monster, study I 1939
  Watercolour, chalk and pencil, 11½ × 16 in. s.l.l.
  Exh: Tooth July 1939 (10)
  Lord Croft
See No.177.

180

180 Woods on the Avon Shore* 1939–46(?)
  Watercolour and chalk, 7¾ × 10¾ in. s. & d.
  1938 l.l.
  Sheffield City Art Galleries

Previously dated 1938, as inscribed on the picture, but stylistically it appears to be a very late work, and it is recorded as delivered to Tooth's only in 1946. The picture shows the Avon Gorge from the Clifton Spa Hotel (see No.176) where the Nashes stayed only once, in March 1939. It was almost certainly made in 1946 (when for much of the time Nash was too unwell to find new subjects) from an earlier outline, and Nash presumably misremembered the date of the Bristol visit when adding '1938'.

181 Pillar and Moon* 1932(?)–40 (repr. on p.30)
  Oil, 20 × 30 in. s.l.r.
  Exh: Tate 1948 (52)
  Tate Gallery, London

The design relates to a photograph Nash took of a pillar in the perimeter wall of Ascott Park, Stadhampton, Oxfordshire (repr. *Paul Nash's Photo-*

graphs, plate 84). The pillar first appeared in Nash's art in a watercolour dated 1929 (15 × 22 in. Private collection), the proper title of which is uncertain, but may be 'Pillar and Avenue', listed in Notebook 1 as of 1929. Two other watercolours showing the pillar are almost identical to the oil. The first (15 × 22 in. Private collection) is hard to date but might be *c*.1937 on grounds of style; the second (6½ × 9½ in. squared. Private collection) is probably, since it is squared, the working drawing for the oil; it is dated 1943, but this certainly refers to the date Nash gave it to the friend whose name is inscribed next to the date. A third watercolour, 'Pillar and Wood' (exh: LG 1932 (27), ex coll: Sir Gerald Barry), has not been seen by the author, but is probably connected.

Nash dated 'Pillar and Moon' 1932–42 for the 1944 Penguin Modern Painters book on his work. He intended to show it as No.24 in his 1938 exhibition at the Leicester Galleries, so it must have been well advanced by then, and he eventually delivered it to Tooth's in 1940. Nash's earlier date points to a connection with 'Pillar and Wood', though in style

the oil painting looks not earlier than 1937. It was bought by the NA–CF in 1940 for presentation to the Tate, and unless Nash took it back from Tooth's between 1940 and 1942, his later date must be wrong.

182 Totes Meer* 1940(?)–41
   Oil, 40 × 60 in. s.l.r.
   Exh: Leeds 1943 (23); Tate 1948 (54)
   Tate Gallery, London

The design was based on a set of photographs Nash made at Cowley dump of wrecked German aircraft near Oxford in August 1940 (two examples repr. *Paul Nash's Photographs*, plates 92 and 93). He described the subject in a letter of 11 March 1941 to Kenneth Clark, chairman of the War Artists' Advisory Committee:

> The thing looked to me suddenly, like a great innundating Sea. You might feel – under certain influences – a moonlight night for instance – this is a vast tide moving across the fields, the breakers rearing up and crashing on the plain. And then, no: nothing moves, it is not water or even ice, it is

something static and dead. It is metal piled up, wreckage. It is hundreds and hundreds of flying creatures which invaded these shores. . . . By moonlight, this waning moon, one could swear they began to move and twist and turn as they did in the air. A sort of rigor mortis? No they are quite dead and still. The only moving creature is the white owl flying low over the bodies of the other predatory creatures, raking the shadows for rats and voles.

Nash developed seven watercolours from the photographs: 'Wreckage Abstraction 1' ($11\frac{1}{2} \times 19$ in. This and others below not located were destroyed in the blitz, May 1941); 'Wreckage Abstraction 2' ($11 \times 7\frac{1}{2}$ in.); 'Wreckage Landscape' (15×22 in. Coll: National Gallery of Canada); 'Wreckage. Lunar Rainbow' (Coll: Leicester Art Gallery, No.189); 'Wreckage Phantom', known also since 1942 as 'Ghost of the Heinkel' ($14\frac{1}{2} \times 22$ in. Coll: Robert McDougall Art Centre, Christchurch, New Zealand); 'Wreckage study 1' (size unknown); 'Wreckage, study 2' (15×22 in. Coll: National Gallery of Canada).

The watercolours were dated 1940 in Tooth's records though they were delivered only in March 1941 at the same time as 'Totes Meer' was sent to the War Artists' Advisory Committee. In the period August 1940–January 1941 Nash was very busy (he delivered two oils and some forty-three watercolours to the WAAC), and, as he had the wreckage photographs, he need not have started either the watercolours or 'Totes Meer' until he was free from his contract with the Air Ministry at the end of 1940.

Nash wrote to Hartley Ramsden shortly after Tooth's was bombed in May 1941: 'Meantime what remains of the drawings are at what remains of Tooth's. . . . They lead up to Dead Sea at the National Gallery. . . . Apart from this there is a set of twelve photographs which I took which are rather extraordinary but no one understands how photography can be used except as a method of cheating (generally associated with the Royal Academy).'

183 Bomber in the Corn 1940
   Watercolour and chalk, $15\frac{1}{2} \times 22\frac{1}{2}$ in. s.l.r. and s. and inscribed with title on the back
   Exh: Leeds 1943 (66)
   Tate Gallery, London
Part of the first set of war pictures that Nash delivered to the War Artists' Advisory Committee in August 1940. Kenneth Clark wrote to Nash that the 'six beautiful watercolours of crashed German aircraft were received with delight by the whole committee'. Nash in 'Picture History' wrote that:

> The fact of their being *out of their element* and being found not among the clouds but in the cornfield or on the moors or stretched across the sands under the cliffs, this had a strong and natural appeal for me. So, for some time, I persisted in my preoccupation of the monster in the fields, although I made other studies of 'planes in flight, but very few quite isolated from the land below.

They went on view at the National Gallery in September. Nos.184, 185 and 187 are part of the same series.

184 Bomber in the Wood* 1940 (repr. on p.30)
   Watercolour and chalk, $15\frac{1}{2} \times 22\frac{3}{8}$ in. s.l.l.
   Exh: New York 1941
   Leeds City Art Galleries
See No.183.

185 Down in the Channel 1940
   Watercolour and chalk, 15×22 in. s.l.l.
   Exh: New York 1941
   South African National Gallery, Cape Town
See No.183.

186 Lebensraum* 1940
   Collage, watercolour and chalk, 15×22 in. s.l.r. and inscribed with title l.l.
   Exh: Zwemmer 1940 (66)
   M. H. Cardiff
The 'trees' are ginkgo leaves and the engraving of a giraffe's skull is from *The Intellectual Observer*, c.1850, and had been used as an illustration to Nash's article, 'The Object', in the *Architectural Review*, October 1936.

187 Raider on the Shore 1940
   Watercolour and chalk, $15\frac{1}{4} \times 22\frac{1}{4}$ in. s.l.l.
   Exh: New York 1941
   Glasgow Art Gallery
See No.183.

188 Tyger, Tyger 1940
   Collage, $4\frac{1}{2} \times 8$ in.
   Mrs Clare Neilson
Nash wrote to Clare Neilson, 12 April 1940, asking 'Did you get a nice collage I sent you at Easter of a tiger eating through a stone wall in the Forest of Dean?'

189 Wreckage. Lunar Rainbow 1940 or 1941
Watercolour and chalk on buff paper,
15¼ × 22¼ in. s.l.l. and inscribed with title on
the back
Exh: Redfern 1942 (15)
Leicester Museums and Art Galleries
See No.182.

190 Battle of Britain* 1941
Oil, 48 × 72 in. s.l.r.
Exh: RA 1945 (88); Tate 1948 (53)
Trustees of the Imperial War Museum, London

A letter to Clare Neilson of 28 June 1941 shows that
Nash was then about to start the painting, which was
commissioned by the Ministry of Information. It
was delivered to the War Artists' Advisory Committee in October and went on view at the National
Gallery in January 1942. He described the work in
'Picture History':

> The painting is an attempt to give the sense of an
> aerial battle in operation over a wide area, and
> thus summarise England's great aerial victory
> over Germany. The scene includes certain ele-
> ments constant during the Battle of Britain – the
> river winding from the town areas across parched
> country, down to the sea; beyond, the shores of
> the continent, above, the mounting cumulus con-
> centrating at sunset after a hot brilliant day, across
> the spaces of sky, trails of airplanes, smoke tracks
> of dead or damaged machines falling, floating
> clouds, parachutes, balloons. Against the ap-
> proaching twilight new formations of the Luft-
> waffe, threatening.
>
> To judge the picture by reference to facts alone
> will be unjust to the experiment. Facts, here, both
> of science and nature are used 'imaginatively' and
> respected only in so far as they suggest symbols
> for the picture plan which itself is viewed as from
> the air. The moment of battle represents the im-
> pact of the opposing forces, the squadrons of the
> R.A.F. sweeping along the coast and breaking up
> a formation of the Luftwaffe while it is still over
> the sea.

Nash used a colour lithograph 'A Thunder-Storm
above Fontainebleau' (Eugene Ciceri, lithographer;
Lemercier, printer; Private collection) in the formation of the composition; it is inscribed '48 × 72' (the
dimensions of the painting) in Nash's hand, top
right. In the oil painting only the river follows the
lithograph closely.

186

190

193

191 Bright Cloud 1941
Watercolour and chalk, $15\frac{1}{2} \times 22\frac{1}{2}$ in. s.l.l.
Exh: Tate 1948 (129)
Lord Croft
One of a set of watercolours, which also includes
Nos.192–4, that resulted from a visit to Madams in
July 1941.

192 Laocoon 1941
Watercolour, chalk and pencil, 11×15 in. s.l.r.
Exh: PN's Camera 1951 (55)
Mrs M. H. Davidson Swift
Related to a photograph reproduced in *Fertile
Image*, plate 35. See No.191.

193 Madamite Moon* 1941
Watercolour and chalk, $11\frac{1}{2} \times 15\frac{1}{2}$ in. s.l.r.
Exh: Redfern October 1941 (14); Tate 1948
(124)
The Viscount Eccles
See No.191.

194 Monster Pond 1941
Watercolour and chalk, $11\frac{1}{2} \times 15\frac{1}{2}$ in. s.l.l.
Exh: London Museum 1942 (7a); Tate 1948
(123)
Richard Smart
See No.191.

195 Don't Forget the Diver c.1941
Collage, watercolour, ink and pencil,
$11 \times 15\frac{1}{4}$ in. Monogram l.r. and inscribed with
title on the back
Exh: Redfern 1942 (44)
*Royal Albert Memorial Museum and Art
Gallery, Exeter*

196 November Moon* 1942 (repr. on p.39)
Oil, 30×20 in. Monogram l.l.
Exh: LG January 1943 (120); Tate 1948 (55)
Fitzwilliam Museum, Cambridge
The view is in the garden of Sandlands at Boars
Hill, Oxford.

197

197 Sunflower and Sun* 1942
Oil, 20 × 30 in. Monogram l.r.
Art Gallery of New South Wales, Sydney (Gift
of the Contemporary Art Society, London)
Delivered by Nash to Tooth's in December 1942.
The view is from Boars Hill, Oxford, overlooking
Bagley Woods.
Nash described the work in 'Picture History':

Thus in the second picture, Sunflower and Sun,
over a scene of wooded landscape dominated by
twin hills, crowned with clumps of dense trees, a
shaft of sunlight breaking through the cloud falls
across the form of a giant sunflower bowed by the
wind. I cannot explain this picture. It means only
what it says. Its design was evolved from the
actual landscape under much the same atmos-
pheric conditions. There was such a sunflower and
some such effect of sunlight. All the elements of
this picture were present in more or less degree.
But the drama of the event, which implies the
mystical association of the sun and the sunflower,
is heightened by the two opposing ellipses and by
the other echoing forms of the sky which retaliate
with the same apparent movement of outspread
wings made by the leaves of the flower.

198 Follow the Führer. Above the Clouds 1942
Watercolour, pencil and collage, $15\frac{1}{4} \times 22\frac{1}{4}$ in.
s. and inscribed with title l.r.
Exh: LG 1942 (8)
Private collection
Part of a set with Nos.199 and 200.

199 Follow the Führer. Over the Snows* 1942
Watercolour, pencil and collage, $15\frac{1}{4} \times 22\frac{1}{4}$ in.
s. and inscribed with title l.r.
Exh: LG 1942 (8)
M. A. Vaughan-Lee
See No.198.

200 Follow the Führer. Under the Waves 1942
Watercolour, pencil and collage, $15\frac{1}{4} \times 22\frac{1}{4}$ in.
s. and inscribed with title l.r.
Exh: LG 1942 (8)
Private collection
See No.198.

201 Landscape of the Malvern Distance 1943
Oil, 22 × 30 in. s.l.l.
Exh: Beaux Arts Gallery 1943; Tate 1948 (58)
Southampton Art Gallery
The last oil painting Nash made of a subject at

199

203

Madams; the view is northwards from Madams to the Malvern Hills.

202 Landscape of the Summer Solstice 1943
Oil, 28 × 36 in. s.l.l.
Exh: Paris 1946 (37)
National Gallery of Victoria, Melbourne

Delivered to Tooth's in October 1943. The view is from Boars Hill, Oxford, overlooking Bagley Woods. Nash gave a description of the work in 'Picture History':

Actually there is nothing to it – the method is . . . taking visual facts in nature for visual use in a picture regardless of natural logic. Objects to me are all the same in the end, i.e. part of a picture, but primarily a pictorial part not merely symbolical. I may hunt out symbolical flowers to make a picture about the Summer Solstice but they must be useful pictorially, namely in colour and form. Thus the presence of the Orpine, a sedum, suggests the introduction of a stone. The queer pink of the flowers and the cold sea-green leaves are just what I want to build up my ochres and deep blues and give me the opportunity of tinting up my foreground of rough grass with a pink glow. Similarly, the flowers of the mouse-eared hawksweed, very much exaggerated, are of great importance to echo the form of the sun and to repeat his image. The tall straight stem of St. John's wort, with its branching fronds and jets of bright yellow petals, makes a significant division where it is absolutely needed. And yet, for all this utility procedure, I am convinced the presence of these magic flowers somehow influences the atmosphere of the picture. That is a mystery, but I believe in it without question and without being able to explain.

203 Landscape of the Vernal Equinox* 1943
Oil, 28 × 36 in. s.l.r.
Exh: Paris & Prague 1945 (28); Tate 1948 (63)
Queen Elizabeth the Queen Mother

The scene is Boars Hill, Oxford, overlooking Bagley Woods. The date is generally given as 1943-4 or 1944, but Tooth's records show that Nash delivered it to them in the summer of 1943. Nash described it in 'Picture History' as follows:

Call it, if you like, a transcendental conception; a landscape of the imagination which has evolved in two ways: on the one hand through a personal interpretation of the phenomenon of the equinox, on the other through the inspiration derived from an actual place. In each case so-called truths of knowledge and appearance have been disregarded where it seemed necessary. Just as probably, it would not be possible to find a period (of day or night) when the sun and moon are in the relationship shown here, so it would be difficult to recognise features of the landscape in the natural scene, a garden of neglected lawns and shrubs leading down into a wood with hills beyond.

The only forms and facts that interest the painter are those which can be used pictorially; these imagination seizes upon and uses in a quite arbitrary way.

The phenomenon of the Spring Equinox, for example, presents the *fact* of equal day and night; which contains the idea of simultaneous sun and moon – a red disc and a white. Again, the thought of division into light and darkness in equal parts suggests a divided space wherein a landscape, on one side, is lit by the setting sun, while the other lies under the influence of a rising moon. This, in turn, determines certain dominant colours. Red and deep yellows, with a range of fading and dying rose and pink, and blue from its palest cold tints, deepening to the tones of night.

It is early spring. The woods are diffused with the glow of buds about to break. There is a beech hedge still in its winter leaf, pure 'rouge Anglais'. The line of rose bushes and the rough grass of the neglected garden are full of ghostly tints, from the mingling beams of sun and moon, where the rival illuminations merge in the sky; and over the distant view, the intermediate pale greens and green-greys and subtleties of brown and blue come into play to complete the full harmony. The design of the composition is largely determined by the important feature of the two central hills crowned by dome-like woods. These are the Wittenham Clumps, part of the Berkshire Downs, an early British stronghold once called Sinodun. Under the trees are long barrows. Below the clumps is the remains of an ancient forest. In the painter's mind this place has a compelling magic which makes it a sympathetic setting for the occasion of the Equinox.

204 Michaelmas Landscape 1943
Oil, 25 × 30 in. s.l.r.
Exh: Paris & Prague 1945 (30); Tate 1948 (57)
Ferens Art Gallery, City of Kingston upon Hull

Delivered to Tooth's in February 1943. The view is from Boars Hill, Oxford, overlooking Bagley Woods.

207

209

205 Landscape of the Vale, Dawn 1943
    Watercolour and pencil, 14 × 21 in. s.l.r.
    Birmingham City Museums and Art Gallery
The view is from Madams towards the Cotswolds.

206 Landscape of the Vale to the South 1943
    Watercolour and pencil, 15½ × 22½ in. s.l.r.
    Exh: Redfern 1961 (12)
    Executors of the late Adam M. Hamilton
The view is from Madams towards the Cotswolds.

207 Maiden Castle* 1943
    Watercolour and chalk, 11¼ × 15½ in. s.l.l.
    Exh: Tate 1948 (110)
    Commander Sir Michael Culme-Seymour, Bt.
Always previously dated 1935, probably on the
grounds that it was connected with the *Dorset Shell
Guide*. But stylistically it is obviously a late work and
the outcome of Nash's trip to Dorset (including
Maiden Castle) in September 1943. He wrote to
Lance Sieveking:

> . . . looking back over the great voyage to the hills
> and the heaths and the sea, it seems all a dream
> but most fortunately a dream remembered – and
> so incredibly varied – I shall never quite get over
> it.

Two other watercolour views of Maiden Castle
exist; 'Hill Architecture' of 1935 (11¼ × 15½ in.
Private collection) and 'Maiden Castle' of 1937
(21½ × 30 in. Coll: Robert Hull Fleming Museum,
University of Vermont). Nash wrote about Maiden
Castle in the *Dorset Shell Guide*:

> Maiden Castle has been described as the largest
> and most perfect earthwork in the world. To say
> it is the finest in Dorset is, perhaps, enough, for in
> no part of any county, I believe – not even in
> Wiltshire, where Avebury stands – can be found
> so complete a sequence of hill architecture. It
> begins where the Ridgeway penetrates Dorset in
> the neighbourhood of Cranborne Chase, through
> the gateway, as it were, of two great earthworks,
> Hambledon Hill and Hod Hill. From that region,
> to the furthest limits of the county, is one vast
> record of ancient occupation. . . . The Maiden is
> in the form of an irregular oval. Its measurements
> are 400 yards wide and 900 yards long. The outer
> circumference amounts to two miles, enclosing an
> area of 130 acres. It is a phenomenon which must
> be seen to be believed if you consider that it was
> constructed throughout a series of occupations,
> the earliest of which can be ascribed to a period
> approaching 2000 B.C.

208 Battle of Germany* 1944
    Oil, 48 × 72 in. s.l.r.
    Exh: RA 1945 (330); Tate 1948 (60)
    Trustees of the Imperial War Museum, London
A sequel to 'Battle of Britain' was commissioned by
the War Artists' Advisory Committee in 1944 and
was originally to have shown the flying bomb. Nash
wrote to Clare Neilson, 5 September 1944, in reply
to a letter of hers in which she described watching
the first flying bomb raid on London, 15–16 June,
from the Savoy Hotel:

> . . . exciting letter of yours. . . . K. Clark wanted
> me to do a sequel to Battle of Britain on the flying
> bomb but it has fallen through I think. I did not
> find any point of departure, no bomb site as it
> were from which to launch into a composition.
> Besides I can think of nothing but my *invasion
> painting* which is now in its critical stage.

The invasion painting, 'Battle of Germany', shows
an allied air attack on a German town, which Nash
described in 'Picture History' as an 'imaginary
scene, but its elements are based on a careful
study of official factual evidence from various
sources'. Kenneth Clark wrote to Nash on behalf of
the WAAC on 3 October to acknowledge its arrival.

Nash gave a description of the painting in 'Picture
History':

> The moment of the picture is when the city lying
> under the uncertain light of the moon awaits the
> blow at her heart. In the background, a gigantic
> column of smoke arises. . . . These two objects,
> pillar and moon, seem to threaten the spent city no
> less than the army of bombers which are about to
> strike out of the red sky. The moon's illumination
> not only reveals the form of the city but, with the
> pillar's increasing width and height, throws its
> largening shadow nearer and nearer. In contrast to
> the waiting city and the quiet though baleful
> moon, the other half of the picture shows the
> opening of the attack. The entire area of sky and
> background and part of the middle distance are
> violently animated. Here forms are used arbi-
> trarily and colour with a kind of chromatic per-
> cussion to suggest explosion and detonation. In
> the central foreground the group of descending
> discs may be a flight of paratroops or the crews of
> aircraft forced to bale out.

209 Flight of the Magnolia* 1944
    Oil 20 × 30 in. s.l.l.
    Exh: Paris & Prague 1945 (29); Tate 1948 (61)
    Commander Sir Michael Culme-Seymour, Bt.

Nash wrote to Clare Neilson, 8 June 1944: 'I am doing some strange new pictures, giant flowers blooming among the clouds or sailing down the night skies like falling stars. These are going to America for a show [Buchholz Gallery, New York, March 1945], but I shall be doing some others now I have got going. Also I have some oil versions of the watercolour designs.' The first watercolours were delivered to Tooth's in June. Nash mentioned them again to Clare Neilson, 5 September 1944: 'I have been doing some new imaginative drawings. Five, including one in colour, are being published in a new magazine Counterpoint, together with an essay by me all to do with aerial flowers.' In his essay 'Aerial Flowers' Nash surveyed his interest in the sky back to his earliest art. It was reissued in booklet form by Counterpoint Publications in 1947. The series includes the watercolours 'Flight of the Magnolia' and 'Nocturnal Flower' (Nos.214 and 216).

Lance Sieveking, in his essay on Nash in *The Eye of the Beholder* (1957), infers that the inspiration for the series was a dawn cloud formation he and Nash saw when they were travelling together in September 1943. But certainly none of the pictures were completed that year.

210 Landscape of the Crescent Moon 1944
    Oil, 20 × 29¾ in. s.l.l.
    Exh: Tooth February 1946 (18)
    Art Gallery of Ontario, Toronto (Gift of Massey
    Foundation 1946)
The view is from Boars Hill over Bagley Woods. The picture was delivered to Tooth's in July 1944.

211 Landscape of the Moon's Last Phase* 1944
    Oil, 25 × 30 in. s.l.l.
    Exh: Cairo & Algiers 1945 (32); Tate 1948 (64)
    Walker Art Gallery, Liverpool
Nash wrote to Dudley Tooth in October 1943 that he was planning a 'Landscape of the Moon's Last Quarter', and again, *c.* January 1944, that he had 'just completed a new painting Landscape of the Moon's Last Phase. . . . It almost winds up that series and is very full blown and frightening'. It was delivered in March 1944. The series as Nash conceived it probably included all the paintings he had made of the garden at Sandlands and the view over Bagley Woods since the autumn of 1942, which would include Nos.196, 197, 202–4, but not 210 which was made four months later.

212 Landscape of the Vernal Equinox 1944
Oil, 25 × 30 in. Unsigned
Exh: Cheltenham 1945 (7)
Scottish National Gallery of Modern Art,
Edinburgh

Among the inscriptions on the stretcher are the title
and '3rd version' in Nash's hand, which indicates
that it is later than No.203 and another painting of
the same title (oil and watercolour, 21¼ × 28¾ in. Ex
coll: Sir Allen Lane) which, like 203, was delivered
to Tooth's in the summer of 1943. Nash painted this
third version specially for his wife and it cannot,
therefore, be dated from Tooth's records, but the
date 1944 given in the 1945 Cheltenham exhibition
catalogue seems likeliest.

213 February Landscape 1944
Watercolour and pencil, 15 × 22 in. s.l.l.
George Mitchell, C.B.E.
The view is from Boars Hill over Bagley Woods.

214 Flight of the Magnolia 1944
Watercolour, chalk and pencil, 11 × 15 in. s.l.r.
Exh: Buchholz 1945 (15)
Santa Barbara Museum of Art (Gift of Wright
Ludington)

One of two near-identical watercolours of the subject, this has frequently been confused with the
other in the Victoria and Albert Museum, which is
on tracing paper and has never been reproduced.
This picture is lightly squared in vertical and horizontal lines, while the squaring on the Victoria and
Albert version also has diagonal lines. See No.209.

215 Midsummer Night, Landscape of the Vale
1944
Watercolour and pencil, 15 × 22 in. s.l.r.
Exh: Tate 1948 (143)
Mr and Mrs G. R. Strauss
The view is from Madams towards the Cotswolds.

216 Nocturnal Flower 1944
Watercolour and chalk, 11½ × 15½ in. s.l.r.
Exh: Buchholz 1945 (12)
Santa Barbara Museum of Art (Gift of Wright
Ludington)
See No.209.

217 Sunset over the Malverns 1944
Watercolour and chalk, 11¾ × 22¾ in. s and
inscribed with title l.l. and d.l.r.
Royal College of Art, London

One of Nash's first views from the Rising Sun Hotel
at Cleeve looking westwards towards the Malverns,
done in October 1944.

218 Winter Country, Landscape of the Vale*
1944
Watercolour, chalk and pencil, 15¼ × 22⅛ in.
s.l.r.
Exh: Cheltenham 1945 (51)
Private collection
A view from Madams to Limbury Hill made on
Nash's last visit to Madams, late February–early
March 1944.

219 Eclipse of the Sunflower 1945
Oil, 28 × 36 in. s.l.l.
Exh: Tate 1948 (68)
British Council

Nash wrote to Lance Sieveking, 2 August 1945:
'There is nothing at the moment, only great schemes
and plans concerning sunflowers and suns.' On
12 November he wrote to Herbert Read: 'I have just
finished the first two large canvases of my sunflower
and sun sequence – two more to come and four accompanying watercolours.' Nash had postponed a
rest stay in the Acland Home, Oxford, in order to
finish this picture and its sequel, 'Solstice of the Sunflower' (No.220). He reported to John Piper from
the Acland Home, 14 November 1945: 'I stipulated
for time to finish my two biggish oils, which I did
last week, and here I am', and to Conrad Aiken,
1 December 1945: 'Do have a look at my two last
paintings [at Tooth's] – perhaps my best.'

In a letter to Dudley Tooth he wrote: 'The
Eclipse explains itself. The withered flower head is a
ghost of the flower in eclipse or just another sunflower time has destroyed and the tempest has torn
up and scattered over the water.'

The whole sequence referred to in the letter to
Read was to include an oil and a watercolour version
of four titles, 'Eclipse of the Sunflower', 'Solstice of
the Sunflower', 'The Sunflower Rises' and 'The
Sunflower Sets'. The other oils in the series were not
painted, and a letter to Richard Smart, a director of
Tooth's, of 25 June 1946, three weeks before Nash's
death, in which he wrote 'So far I have not re-embarked upon oil painting' (after his serious illness at
the beginning of the year) indicates that this and
No.220 may have been his last oils.

220 Solstice of the Sunflower* 1945
Oil, 28 × 36 in. Monogram and s.l.l.
Exh: Tooth February 1946 (23); Tate 1948 (67)
National Gallery of Canada, Ottawa

218

See No.219. In a letter to Dudley Tooth he wrote: Four pictures in which the image of the Sun-flower is exalted to take the part of the Sun. In three of the pictures the flower stands in the sky in place of the Sun. But in the 'Solstice' the spent sun shines from its zenith encouraging the sun-flower in the dual role of sun and firewheel to per-form its mythological purpose. The sun appears to be whipping the sunflower like a top. The Sun-flower Wheel tears over the hill cutting a path through the standing corn and bounding into the air as it gathers momentum. This is the blessing of the Midsummer Fire.

221 Clouds, Hill and the Plain 1945
Watercolour and pencil, $11\frac{1}{4} \times 15\frac{1}{2}$ in. d.l.l.
Exh: Redfern 1961 (24)
Lord Croft

222

One of the last set of watercolours made at Cleeve in June 1945.

222 Flower Resting in the Landscape* 1945
Watercolour and pencil, 15 × 22 in. s. & d.
'45 l.l.
Exh: Tooth 1945 (2); Tate 1948 (150)
Private collection

From a set of at least sixteen watercolours made from Cleeve Hill during the Nashes' Christmas–New Year stay 1944–5; others are Nos.223–31.

223 Landscape Emerging 1945
Watercolour and chalk, $11\frac{1}{2} \times 15\frac{1}{2}$ in.
Monogram l.r.
Exh: Tooth 1945 (14)
Guy H. Dixon
See No.222.

235

224 The Landscape Fading 1945
Watercolour and pencil, $11 \times 15\frac{1}{2}$ in. s.l.l.
Miss Evelyn Higgins
See No.222.

225 The Landscape under Mist and Frost 1945
Watercolour and pencil, $15\frac{1}{2} \times 22\frac{1}{2}$ in.
Exh: Tooth 1945 (15)
National Gallery of Victoria, Melbourne
See No.222.

226 The Sun Descending, study 3 1945
Watercolour and chalk, 11¼ × 15½ in.
Monogram l.r.
Exh: Tooth 1945 (18); Tate 1948 (145)
Mrs Broke Freeman
See No.222.

227 The Sun Descending, study 4 1945
Watercolour and pencil, 11 × 15½ in.
Monogram l.l.
Exh: Tooth 1945 (11)
Private collection
See No.222.

228 The Sun Descending, study 5 1945
Watercolour and chalk, 11¼ × 15½ in.
Monogram l.l.
Exh: Tooth 1945 (5); Tate 1948 (146)
Private collection
See No.222.

229 The Sun Descending, study 6 1945
Watercolour and pencil, 11¼ × 15½ in.
Monogram l.l.
Exh: Tooth 1945 (1); Tate 1948 (147)
Private collection
See No.222.

230 The Sun Descending, study 7* 1945
(repr. on p.40)
Watercolour and chalk, 11¾ × 15¼ in. s.l.r.
Exh: Tate 1948 (148)
Private collection
See No.222.

231 Sunset Eye, study 2 1945
Watercolour, 11½ × 15½ in. s.l.r.
Exh: Tate 1948 (149)
Lord Croft
See No.222.

232 Landscape of the Vale, Gloucestershire
1945–6
Watercolour, oil, chalk and pencil on paper,
22 × 30 in. Unsigned
Oldham Art Gallery
A view from Cleeve Hill, which was given this title
by Margaret Nash in 1953. Though Cleeve is in
Gloucestershire, Nash himself reserved the assig-
nation 'Landscape of the Vale' for pictures painted
from Madams, so the title is not strictly authentic.

The combination of media is unique in Nash's

work, though there is one example of a painting that
is chiefly oil with some watercolour ('Landscape of
the Vernal Equinox', second version, 21¼ × 28¾ in.
Ex coll: Sir Allen Lane). Margaret Nash described
this as Paul's 'last big landscape' by which she must
have meant larger than his standard large paper size
(15 × 22 in.), because Nash did not visit Cleeve after
June 1945 and his last standard large watercolours
were the Isle of Wight series (see No.234).

233 Eclipse of the Sunflower* 1946(?)
(repr. on p.40)
Watercolour and pencil, 16½ × 22½ in. Unsigned
Exh: OAC 1949 (32)
Victoria and Albert Museum, London
Always previously dated 1945 except in the Oxford
Arts Club 1949 catalogue, where it is dated 1946.
The later date is probable in view of Nash's letter to
Herbert Read of 12 November 1945 showing that
the oil paintings of sunflowers preceded the watercolours (see No.219). Nash wrote to Richard Smart,
25 June 1946: 'So far I have not re-embarked upon
oil painting [after his serious illness at the beginning
of the year]. Nor have I made any headway with the
large watercolours. I was obliged to tear up the
bouncing sunflower. It wasn't good enough. The
only complete one is the eclipsed sunflower as good
as any of the series so far.' The 'bouncing sunflower'
must refer to the watercolour version of 'Solstice of
the Sunflower' (the oil is No.220) which was never
remade. Nash was clearly considering the sunflower
problem less than three weeks before his death on
11 July but the letter to Smart does not date this
picture exactly. See No.237.

234 Landscape, Isle of Wight, study 1 1946
Watercolour and chalk, 14¾ × 20¾ in. Unsigned
Exh: LG 1953 (23)
David H. Nash, M.B.E.
From a set of three watercolours Nash made from
the balcony of his room at the Florida Hotel,
Boscombe, Hampshire, looking towards the Isle of
Wight; they are the last pictures he made. The
others are in private collections, but the watercolour
in the Victoria and Albert Museum known as 'Land-
scape, Isle of Wight, study 2' is a landscape from
Madams with a distant view of Gloucester Cathedral.

235 Landscape of the Vegetable Kingdom* 1946
Watercolour, chalk and pencil, 9 × 13¾ in. s.l.l.
Exh: LG 1953 (43)
Mrs Peter Timms

236 Landscape of the Wittenham Clumps 1946
Watercolour, chalk and pencil, 6⅜ × 9¾ in. s.l.r.
Exh: Newcastle 1971 (46)
Dr Richard Seddon

237 The Sunflower Rises 1946
Watercolour and pencil, 17 × 22½ in. Unsigned
Exh: Hamet 1973 (68)
Scottish National Gallery of Modern Art,
Edinburgh

Nash's letter to Richard Smart of 25 June 1946 (see
No.233) shows that this was not then finished, which
suggests that Nash worked on it between then and
his departure for Boscombe on 3 July. The wall on
the right belongs to the garden of the Nashes' home
at 106 Banbury Road, Oxford.

238 Found Objects
a–e Objects used by Nash in some of his works

a Porcelain doll's head
   Private collection
Used in the paintings 'Environment for Two Ob-
jects' (No.158) and 'Changing Scene' (No.162).

b Horn
   Nash Trustees
Used in the object 'Encounter of the Wild Horns'
(No.170e) and painted in 'Nocturnal Landscape'
(No.171).

c Hull of a toy boat
   Paul Nash Trustees
Used in the object 'The Archer' (No.170b).

d Ivory hand
   Private collection
Used in the object 'Victorian Paradox' (No.170h).

e Ivory spindle with hands
   Private collection

220

Chronology

1889
Paul Nash born in London on 11 May, son of William Harry Nash, a barrister, and Caroline Maude Nash

1898
Nash sent to Colet Court, the preparatory school for St. Paul's, in January.

1901
The Nashes moved to Wood Lane House which had been specially built for them at Iver Heath in Buckinghamshire, the county where the family are recorded as landowners and farmers back to the sixteenth century. Paul became a boarder at Colet Court.

1903
Went to St. Paul's in the autumn, but transferred to a cram school in January 1904 in order to gain entry to the Navy; he subsequently failed the exam and returned to St. Paul's.

1906
Left St. Paul's in July; registered for art classes at Chelsea Polytechnic in December.

1907
Probably started making bookplates in this year; he made many up to 1910, and a few later.

1908
In the autumn transferred from Chelsea to the London County Council School at Bolt Court off Fleet Street. His devotion to Rossetti began about now, and lasted till around the middle of 1911. In the catalogue of his 1924 exhibition at the Leicester Galleries Nash dated his beginnings as an artist to this year.

1909–10
Nash's work was singled out for praise by William Rothenstein at a Bolt Court competition. Rothenstein became Nash's strongest early champion, and they remained lifelong friends.

1910
Death of Nash's mother on 14 February at the age of 49 after a long illness. In April the beginning of Nash's correspondence with the poet and playwright Gordon Bottomley, which was to last with a break (1932–8) till

Nash's death. Nash made his first trip abroad, to Normandy and Brittany with relations, for about a fortnight from 31 August. In October Nash registered at the Slade and at first did four days a week drawing from the antique, but in December was admitted to the life class for two days. At first he was very enthusiastic about the Slade, but by February 1911 was depressed by his lack of success at figure drawing.

1911
Friendship with Ben Nicholson, fellow student at the Slade. Nash visited Nicholson's home at Rottingdean in April, and Ben paid a return visit to Iver Heath in June. That summer Nash concentrated more on landscape drawings in which he was encouraged by another Slade friend, Claughton Pellew-Harvey. In July he first met Mrs Harry Taylor, who lived at Iver Heath and gave him an introduction to the painter Sir William Richmond; Richmond later (probably summer 1912) encouraged Nash to develop the landscape side of his art. In October Nash took a room at Paultons Square in Chelsea, which he kept until May 1912 when he returned to live at Iver Heath. In December he left the Slade.

1912
In April Nash seems to have returned to Bolt Court for classes in figure drawing, perhaps only for a very short time. In September he probably made his first drawings of Wittenham Clumps during his family's annual visit to Sinodun, Berkshire, to stay with relations. In November he had his first one-man exhibition, at the Carfax Gallery, to whose manager, A. B. Clifton, he had been given an introduction by Richmond. Rothenstein was one of the buyers. In December he had a brief holiday at Mundesley on the Norfolk coast with Pellew-Harvey and drew 'The Cliff to the North'. In December he first met Bottomley, at the home of Robert Trevelyan in Surrey.

1913
In February a Slade friend, Rupert Lee, introduced Nash to his future wife, Margaret Theodosia Odeh, daughter of the chaplain to the Anglican bishop of Jerusalem, a scholar and graduate of St. Hilda's College, Oxford, and a suffragette; they were engaged in April. Margaret lived in Queen Alexandra Mansions, Judd Street, near St. Pancras Station, and the Nashes kept a flat in the block until 1936.

In April Nash called on Yeats and proposed a set of

illustrations to Yeats's *The Wind among the Reeds* (1899), but nothing came of the scheme. He first showed at the New English Art Club in May, and, according to Robert Trevelyan reported by Bottomley, Roger Fry found Nash's pictures there the best in the show. Nash first met Fry in November when Fry came to see the joint exhibition of Paul and his brother John at the Dorien Leigh Gallery in South Kensington. Charles Rutherston and Michael Sadler bought the first of the many Paul Nashes in their collections at this exhibition. In December Spencer Gore took six Paul Nashes for his English Post-Impressionists exhibition at Brighton.

1914
Nash held in high esteem by Fry: in February he joined the Omega Workshops, and several times during the first half of the year worked with Fry on the restoration of the Mantegna frescoes at Hampton Court. In February he showed for the first time, as a member, at the Friday Club, which was within Fry's orbit of influence. Also in February his brother John introduced him to Edward Marsh who, in the course of some thirty years, was to buy many of his pictures for himself and the Contemporary Art Society. Marsh introduced him to Siegfried Sassoon and the 'tramp poet' W. H. Davies, who was to become a buyer, in March, and in July to Rupert Brooke. Nash was closely involved with Marsh in his plan for the book 'Georgian Drawings' planned as a sequel to *Georgian Poetry*, which Marsh had edited. In May Nash was represented in the exhibition *Twentieth-century Art: a Review of the Modern Movements* at the Whitechapel Art Gallery. In July he and Margaret visited the Bottomleys at their home in north Lancashire and subsequently toured the Lake District, visiting the collections of Michael Sadler in Leeds and Charles Rutherston in Manchester on their way home.

On 10 September Nash enlisted for home defence. 14 December, Paul and Margaret were married at St. Martin-in-the-Fields; they spent their honeymoon in Somerset.

1915
1 January, in barracks at Roehampton. First showed at the London Group in March, as a non-member. December, guarding the Tower of London.

1916
May, a map-reading instructor at Romford, Essex, where he met the poet Edward Thomas. In August started officer training at Denham, and in September at Camberley. Gazetted second-lieutenant on 19 December, and assigned to the third battalion, Hampshire Regiment.

1917
Reached France 22 February, and after some days at Rouen arrived in the Ypres Salient early in March; apart from attending a short training course at the end of April, Nash remained in the front or reserve line till he broke a rib in a fall on 25 May, and was invalided home. It was a quiet period at the front and Nash saw no serious fighting.

Returned to England 30 May, and was in hospital at Cosham, Hants; then lived at Gosport. One-man exhibition of war drawings at the Goupil Gallery in June, and one including war and non-war pictures at the Birmingham Repertory Theatre in September, organised by John Drinkwater, who became an important new patron. In July Nash met C. R. W. Nevinson who had been making war pictures since 1914; Nevinson helped Nash to learn lithography, Nash completing his first lithograph at the end of December.

On 12 October Nash was seconded to the Department of Information under John Buchan with the prospect of appointment as an Official Artist at the Front, having been strongly recommended by many leading art world figures, including Fry, Marsh, Rothenstein and Sadler. Left for the Ypres Salient as an Official Artist on 31 October; spent most of November there drawing the immediate aftermath of the Battle of Passchendaele, and then about a week working for the Canadian war records at Vimy in France, before returning to England on 7 December.

1918
First official war drawings published in *Country Life*, 15 January, and a book of colour reproductions in the *Country Life* series 'British Artists at the Front' published soon after. In April received the commission from the Ministry of Information for the large oil painting 'The Menin Road'. His exhibition *Void of War* at the Leicester Galleries in May included his earliest surviving oil paintings. Spent the summer and autumn working on 'The Menin Road' in a studio at Chalfont St. Peter, Bucks, which he shared with John Nash.

1919
Finished 'The Menin Road' in a studio in Gower Street in January; released from war artist's service 12 February, and discharged from the army 13 February. Spent that year partly in London and partly at Whiteleaf in the Chilterns, and first visited Dymchurch on the Kent Coast where he was soon to settle. Made his first wood engravings. Between April and November wrote art criticism for the *New Witness*, partly under the pseudonym Robert Derriman. In November organised a one-man exhibition in a studio at 9 Fitzroy Street which he had been lent by the painter Wyndham Tryon; reviews of this show included the first assessment of Nash, in *The Athenaeum*, 5 December 1919, by R. H. Wilenski, who was to remain Nash's most consistent critical champion, and was finally to write that 'Paul Nash, . . . in my judgement, is the greatest English artist of my time' (*World Review*, January 1946).

1920

J. M. Barrie's *The Truth about the Russian Dancers* produced at the Coliseum in March with sets and costumes by Nash; this was the only actual production Nash was involved in though he did a considerable amount of design work for the theatre, mainly in the early 1920s. In April he visited Leeds with John Nash to gather material for mural paintings to have been made for Leeds Town Hall; the scheme was organised by William Rothenstein on behalf of Michael Sadler, Vice-Chancellor of Leeds University, and the artists involved were the Nashes, Jacob Kramer, Albert Rutherston, Stanley Spencer and Edward Wadsworth; but the murals were not carried out. The summer was spent at Dymchurch, and in October Nash started his first teaching job, at an art school in Oxford run by Albert Rutherston.

1921

Spent the summer at Dymchurch at 2 Rose Cottages; close friendship with Claude Lovat Fraser, who suddenly died in July. On a visit to Iver Heath in September Nash was shocked to find his father unconscious and at first thought him dead; shortly afterwards Nash himself collapsed and was unconscious for a week in the London Hospital for Nervous Diseases; his condition was diagnosed as suppressed war strain.

1922

In May Nash first visited Percy Withers who was to be a lifelong friend and patron. In September T. E. Lawrence visited Nash and commissioned designs to be made from photographs for what was to be the private edition of *The Seven Pillars of Wisdom. A Triumph* (1926). Lawrence, an old acquaintance of Margaret Nash, since he had learned Arabic in Oxford from her father, had bought an oil painting 'Coast Scene' (1920) which, after he left the Colonial Office, hung for a time at the Tate, the first of Nash's pictures to be shown there. Nash's friendship with Lawrence lasted till the latter's death in 1936. In December the Nashes visited Paris, probably for the first time, staying at the Hôtel Voltaire near the Pont Royale. Also in December Nash's *Places*, a set of landscape wood engravings with accompanying texts by the artist, was published by Heinemann.

1923

The Nashes moved to a larger house at Dymchurch, Pantile Cottage on the road to Lydd. First monograph on Nash's work published in the series 'Contemporary British Artists' (Ernest Benn), with an introduction by Anthony Bertram.

1924

In May Nash had a major exhibition at the Leicester Galleries, planned since 1921 but postponed, and successful in terms of sales. In July Nash visited Ben and Winifred Nicholson at Brampton in Cumberland, a return visit for one the Nicholsons had made to Dymchurch the previous year. Published a series of wood engravings illustrating the first chapter of *Genesis* (Nonesuch Press). In September appointed assistant in the school of design at the Royal College of Art. In December went to Paris and again stayed at the Hôtel Voltaire.

1925

From Paris travelled to Cros de Cagnes, staying at the Pension de la Plage, then in March visited Genoa, Pisa, Florence and Siena, admiring especially Sienese painting. Returned to England in April, and shortly afterwards left Dymchurch and moved to Oxenbridge Cottage, Iden near Rye, which the Nashes rented from Bertram Buchanan whom they had known since about 1920. In July Nash gave up his job at the R.C.A. One-man exhibition of watercolours at the Mayor Gallery in November.

1927

Elected to the London Artists Association in January. One-man exhibition of watercolours at the Warren Gallery in May. Made the first of a series of pictures of the view from his London flat towards St. Pancras Station.

1928

A brief visit to Normandy in June, taking in Caen and Rouen. A retrospective exhibition of wood engravings at the Redfern Gallery in July, and a major exhibition of new paintings at the Leicester Galleries in November, including the first pictures to mark the beginning of a decisive change in his art.

1929

The death of Nash's father on 27 February.

1930

In late February the Nashes left for a holiday in the south of France with the painter Edward Burra and their friend Ruth Clark. They went first to Paris and visited Léonce Rosenberg's Gallery where Nash saw a large collection of contemporary French painting for the first time; they then stayed at Toulon and visited Marseilles, Nice and Cros de Cagnes, returning to England in mid-April. In December the Nashes moved from Iden to New House, Rye, which had a view from the back across Romney Marsh towards the sea. In the same month Nash became art critic for the *Weekend Review* (till June 1933), and in April 1931 became art critic of *The Listener* in conjunction with Herbert Read (writing regularly till September 1932 and then occasionally till May 1935).

1931
Visited the United States as English judge on the jury of the Carnegie International Award, Pittsburgh. Left England with his wife, 12 September; they were shown public and private art collections in New York, Washington and Philadelphia before being taken to Pittsburgh, but saw contemporary American art in New York only briefly before returning home in mid-October. His wife gave him a camera for the trip, and images taken from photographs, which had first appeared in his work in 1929, became increasingly common from this year. In October Nash had his first retrospective exhibition of pictures at the Oxford Arts Club.

1932
Nash's most important book illustrations, for Sir Thomas Browne's *Urne Buriall and The Garden of Cyrus*, published by Cassell, and *Room and Book*, a collection of essays on aspects of design, published by the Soncino Press. Elected President and Chairman of the Society of Industrial Artists (resigned 1934).

1933
In January suffered a serious attack of bronchitis which had first affected him in 1930, and spent most of April having treatment at Tunbridge Wells; his bronchial condition was chronic from this time. On 12 June *The Times* published Nash's letter announcing the formation of the Unit One group of painters, sculptors and architects; Nash had got the idea for the group from Tooth's exhibition in October 1931, *Recent Developments in British Painting*, for which he had helped to select the contributors, and he worked subsequently on the formation of the group with Henry Moore.

In July the Nashes sold their house at Rye, and Paul went with Ruth Clark to stay at Marlborough because he wanted to revisit Savernake Forest where he had painted in 1925 and 1927; the most important result was his discovery of Avebury, which remained a source of inspiration until 1938. In November the Nashes left for Paris and the Riviera.

1934
In January and February the Nashes were at the Hôtel des Princes in Nice, where for some of the time Paul was ill; in April they went to Marseilles and briefly visited Gibraltar, Spain and North Africa, returning to England in June. Nash missed the London exhibition of Unit One, which opened at the Mayor Gallery on 10 April, coinciding with the publication of the book *Unit One* (Cassell), which was edited by Herbert Read and included reproductions and statements by the artists; the exhibition travelled till early 1935 to Liverpool, Manchester, Hanley, Derby, Swansea and Belfast.

The Nashes spent the summer in rented houses on Romney Marsh; they met for the first time Charles and Clare Neilson who were to become close friends. Nash

discovered his first 'found object', 'Marsh Personage'; found objects were commonly included in his paintings up to 1938. In October the Nashes moved to Dorset to Whitecliff Farm outside Swanage below Ballard Down, which they were lent by the Felce family whom they had met on the Riviera in 1925.

1935
In February the Nashes moved from Whitecliff to rooms in Swanage at 2 The Parade. They spent most of the year there, and Paul collected material for the *Dorset Shell Guide* (1936) which he compiled and edited. In the summer he consulted the architect F. R. S. Yorke with a view to having a house built at Swanage, but soon abandoned the idea. Nash probably started work in this year on his autobiography, a chapter of which was published in *Signature*, July 1938; the full text appeared only posthumously (Faber 1949).

1936
In March the Nashes left Swanage, and only visited Dorset briefly thereafter; they bought a house at 3 Eldon Grove in Hampstead, which they moved into in the autumn. Nash was a committee member of and exhibitor at the *International Surrealist Exhibition* which opened at the New Burlington Galleries in June, and later showed at other international Surrealist exhibitions in Tokyo (1937), Amsterdam (1938) and Paris (1938).

1937
Visited Dorset in September.

1938
From January till November 1940 was assistant in the school of design at the R.C.A., but taught only till the outbreak of war. In May had his first major exhibition of oil paintings for ten years, at the Leicester Galleries, and had a retrospective at the Venice Biennale. In June he visited Madams, the Neilsons' new home in Gloucestershire, which was to be a major source of inspiration for his late work.

1939
Visited Bristol in March and drew a series of pictures of the Avon Gorge. In April was in Wales, went to see the Misses Davies at the Gregynog Press at Newtown, Montgomeryshire, and on to Aberystwyth. In August the Nashes left London and took rooms in Oxford in Beaumont Street. In October Nash opened the Arts Bureau for War Service in Oxford, which was designed to make constructive use of artists in war activities.

1940
In March Nash was appointed an official war artist by the War Artists' Advisory Committee, and worked for the Air Ministry until December. After considering moving to Bath or Bristol the Nashes took a flat at 106

Banbury Road, Oxford, in June. In July Nash set up a canvas 10 × 15 ft, in a studio provided by the Air Ministry in Woburn Square, but it is doubtful whether he worked on it.

1941

Transferred from the Air Ministry to the Ministry of Information in January, Nash very much reduced his output of war pictures. He made two visits to Madams, in late May and late June–early July, which each gave him inspiration for a series of watercolours.

1942

Nash visited Hungerford, where he met a cousin, Nell Bethell whom he had not seen for many years; he subsequently returned there several times up to 1945. In October he was at Madams, and in November made his first paintings at Sandlands, Boar's Hill, just outside Oxford, the home of his friend Hilda Harrisson; from the garden he could see Wittenham Clumps with the help of field glasses. Sandlands was the most important inspiration for late pictures, especially oils.

1943

In April Nash visited Leeds at the time of a retrospective of his work at Temple Newsam House; he stayed with the painter Richard Seddon at Sheffield and made water-colours in Derbyshire. He visited Madams in April and June, Hungerford in August, and in September made his first trip to Dorset since before the war with his friend Lance Sieveking with whom he had served in the First World War; they visited Maiden Castle, Dorchester, Cerne Abbas and the Isle of Portland.

1944

In February Nash made his last series of watercolours at Madams. In October he spent three weeks at the Rising Sun Hotel, Cleeve, near Cheltenham, where he was able to paint the view across the Severn Valley towards the Malverns from inside the hotel. The Nashes went to Cleeve again for Christmas and stayed into the new year.

1945

In March a group of his new watercolours was shown at the Buchholz Gallery, New York; in June he had a retrospective at Cheltenham Art Gallery which he visited from Cleeve. Between August and November he painted what were probably his last oils, 'Eclipse of the Sunflower' and 'Solstice of the Sunflower'.

1946

In January Nash had pneumonia from which he never fully recovered. He died on holiday at Boscombe, Hants, on 11 July.

Exhibitions

1912 November
Drawings by Paul Nash. Carfax & Co.

1913 November
Drawings by Paul Nash. Dorien Leigh Gallery.

1913 December
The Camden Town Group and Others. Brighton Art Gallery.

1914 May
20th Century Art: a Review of the Modern Movements. Whitechapel Art Gallery.

1917 June
Drawings made in the Ypres Salient by Paul Nash. Goupil Gallery.

1917 September
Drawings by Paul Nash. Birmingham Repertory Theatre.

1918 May
Void of War: an Exhibition of Pictures by Lieut. Paul Nash. Leicester Galleries.

1919 November
Drawings by Paul Nash. 9 Fitzroy Street.

1919 December
The Nation's War Paintings and other Records. Royal Academy.

1924 June
Paintings and Watercolours by Paul Nash. Leicester Galleries.

1925 November
[Watercolours by Paul Nash.] Mayor Gallery.

1926 June
Venice Biennale.

1927 February
Exhibition of Paintings, Pastels, Drawings and Woodcuts illustrating Col. T. E. Lawrence's book 'Seven Pillars of Wisdom'. Leicester Galleries.

1927 May
Recent Watercolours and Drawings by Paul Nash. Warren Gallery.

1927 June
Young Artists Exhibition organised by the *Daily Express*. R.B.A. Gallery.

1927 November
2nd exhibition of the London Artists Association. Leicester Galleries.

1928 November
Paintings and Watercolours by Paul Nash. Leicester Galleries.

1929 October
Contemporary British Art including the Collection of Edward Marsh. Whitechapel Art Gallery.

1931 October
Retrospective Exhibition of Work by Paul Nash 1910–1931. Oxford Arts Club.

1931 October
Recent Developments in British Painting. Arthur Tooth & Sons.

1932 June
Venice Biennale.

1932 November
Watercolours by Paul Nash. Leicester Galleries.

1933 October
Art Now. Mayor Gallery.

1934 April
[Contemporary Art.] 34 Gallery.

1934 April
Unit One. Mayor Gallery and provincial tour.

1935 April
Paul Nash. Redfern Gallery.

1935
Artists International Association against Fascism.

1936 June
International Surrealist Exhibition. New Burlington Galleries.

1937 April
Watercolours, Drawings, Collages and Objects by Paul Nash. Redfern Gallery.

1937 April
Artists International Association, Surrealist Section.

1937 September
Surrealist Objects and Poems. London Gallery.

1938 May
New Paintings by Paul Nash. Leicester Galleries.

1938 June
Venice Biennale.

1939 January
Living Art in England. London Gallery.

1939 July
Oils, Watercolours and Exhibits by Paul Nash. Gordon Fraser Gallery, Cambridge.

1939 July
New Paintings by Paul Nash. Arthur Tooth & Sons.

1940 June
Surrealism Today. Zwemmer Gallery.

1940
British Painting since Whistler. National Gallery.

1941
Six British Watercolour Painters of To-Day. National Gallery.

1941
Britain at War. Museum of Modern Art, New York.

1942 March
New Movements in Art: Contemporary Work in England. London Museum.

1942 April
Imaginative Painting since the War. Leicester Galleries.

1942 May
New Movements in Art. Leicester Art Gallery.

1942 June
Paul Nash, New Watercolours and others of various dates. Redfern Gallery.

1943 June
Paintings and Drawings by Paul Nash. Temple Newsam House, Leeds.

1945 March
Contemporary British Artists. Buchholz Gallery, New York.

1945 April
New Watercolours by Paul Nash. Arthur Tooth & Sons.

1945 June
Paintings, Drawings and Designs by Paul Nash. Cheltenham Art Gallery.

1945 October
National War Pictures, organised by the War Artists' Advisory Committee. Royal Academy.

1945
Contemporary British Art. British Council. Paris & Prague.

1945
Contemporary British Art. British Council. Cairo & Algiers.

1946 November
Exhibition of International Modern Art, organised by UNESCO at the Musée d'Art Moderne, Paris.

1948 March
Paul Nash. A Memorial Exhibition. Organised by the Tate Gallery and the Arts Council, Tate Gallery and provincial tour.

1949 February
Watercolours and Drawings by Paul Nash. Oxford Arts Club at Black Hall, Oxford.

1949
Paul Nash 1889–1946. Arts Council touring exhibition of Canada.

1951 November
Paul Nash's Camera. Arts Council Gallery and provincial tour.

1953 May
Paul Nash: a Private Collection of Watercolours and Drawings [Margaret Nash's collection]. Leicester Galleries.

1958
Paintings and Watercolours by Paul Nash from the Collections of Mrs Paul Nash and Mrs Michael Dawnay. St. Hilda's College, Oxford.

1962 June
Paul Nash. Holburne of Menstrie Museum, Bath.

1962 October
British Art and the Modern Movement. Arts Council Exhibition at the National Museum of Wales, Cardiff.

1965 March
Art in Britain 1930–1940. Marlborough Fine Art.

1970 March
Paul Nash 1889–1946. Hamet Gallery.

1971 September
Paul Nash 1889–1946. Northern Arts Gallery, Newcastle upon Tyne.

1973 May
Paul Nash's Photographs. Document and Image. Tate Gallery.

1973 May
Paul Nash 1889–1946. Drawings and Watercolours. Hamet Gallery.

1974 July
Paul Nash 1889–1946. Scottish National Gallery of Modern Art.

1974 August
Art Then. Arts Council Gallery, Edinburgh.

Bibliography

Paul Nash's personal papers are in the Tate Gallery Archive. They include three notebooks, *c.*1928–46, referred to as 'Notebook 1' etc.

Writings by Paul Nash
not including exhibition reviews

'Unit One. A New Group of Artists', letter (dated 2 June) to *The Times*, published 12 June 1933.

'Unit One', *The Listener*, 5 July 1933.

Contribution to *Unit One*, ed. Herbert Read, 1934.

'For, But Not With', *Axis*, January 1935.

Dorset Shell Guide, introduction and gazetteer, Architectural Press [1936].

'Swanage or Seaside Surrealism', *Architectural Review*, April 1936.

'The Object', *Architectural Review*, November 1936.

'Personal View', *Manchester Evening News*, 12 February 1937.

'A Characteristic', *Architectural Record* (New York), March 1937.

'The Life of the Inanimate Object', *Country Life*, 1 May 1937.

Introduction to the catalogue of his exhibition at the Redfern Gallery, April 1937.

'Unseen Landscapes', *Country Life*, 21 May 1938.

'The Giant's Stride', *Architectural Review*, September 1939.

'The Personality of Planes', *Vogue*, March 1942.

'Picture History', notes on his work from 1933 to 1945 prepared for his dealers, Arthur Tooth & Sons, 1943–5. Unpublished, but quoted from by Anthony Bertram in *Paul Nash. The Portrait of an Artist*.

Monster Field. A Discovery Recorded, Counterpoint Publications, Oxford, 1946.

Aerial Flowers, Counterpoint Publications, Oxford, 1947.

Outline. An Autobiography and Other Writings, Faber, 1949.

Poet and Painter. Being the Correspondence of Gordon Bottomley and Paul Nash, ed. C. C. Abbott and Anthony Bertram, Oxford University Press, 1955.

Writings on or concerning Paul Nash

Aiken, Conrad, *Ushant*, W. H. Allen, 1963.

Armstrong, John, 'The Present Tendency of Paul Nash', *Apollo*, November 1932.

Bertram, Anthony, *Paul Nash*, Benn, 1923.

Bertram, Anthony, 'Paul Nash', *The Fleuron*, 1927.

Bertram, Anthony, 'Paul Nash', *Architectural Review*, October 1932.

Bertram, Anthony, 'The Art of Paul Nash', *The Listener*, 9 November 1932.

Bertram, Anthony, *Paul Nash. The Portrait of an Artist*, Faber, 1955. Text references to Bertram refer to this.

Causey, Andrew, introduction to *Paul Nash 1889–1946*, Newcastle exhibition catalogue, September 1971.

Causey, Andrew, introduction to *Paul Nash's Photographs. Document and Image*, Tate Gallery, 1973.

Duveen, Sir Joseph, 'Twenty Years of British Painting', *Studio*, 1930.

Eates, Margot (ed), *Paul Nash. Paintings, Drawings and Illustrations*, Lund Humphries, 1948.

Eates, Margot, *Paul Nash, Master of the Image*, Murray, 1973.

Evans, Myfanwy, 'The Significance of Paul Nash', *Architectural Review*, September 1947.

Fletcher, John Gould, 'Paul Nash', *The Arts* (New York), October 1928.

Gaunt, William, 'Paul Nash', *Drawing and Design*, October 1926.

Grigson, Geoffrey, 'A Metaphysical Artist', *The Listener*, 1 April 1948.

Grigson, Geoffrey, 'Paul Nash', *Vogue*, April 1948.

Harrison, Charles, 'Abstract Painting in Britain in the early 1930s', *Studio*, April 1967.

Heron, Patrick, *The Changing Forms of Art*, Routledge, 1953.

Laver, James, *Portraits in Oil and Vinegar*, Castle, 1925.

Lintott, E. Bernard, *The Art of Watercolour Painting*, Chapman and Hall, 1926.

Nash, Margaret, 'Memoir of Paul Nash 1913–1946', ms. in the Victoria and Albert Museum Library, partly published in *Oxford Magazine*, 5 February 1959.

Nash, Margaret (ed.), *Fertile Image* [Paul Nash's photographs], Faber, 1951.

Newton, Eric, introduction to *Paul Nash. A Memorial Exhibition* catalogue, Tate Gallery, March 1948.

Piper, John, *British Romantic Artists*, Collins, 1942.

Postan, Alexander, *The Complete Graphic Work of Paul Nash*, Secker and Warburg, 1973.

Ramsden, Hartley, 'Surrealism in Landscape', *Country Life*, 2 January 1942.

Ramsden, Hartley, 'Paul Nash as a Landscape Painter', in Eates (ed.) *Paul Nash . . .*, 1948.

Read, Herbert, introduction to *Unit One*, Cassell, 1934.

Read, Herbert, *Paul Nash*, Soho Gallery, 1937.

Read, Herbert, *Paul Nash*, Penguin, 1944.

Read, Herbert, 'Paul Nash, A Modern Romantic', *Picture Post*, 10 April 1948.

Rothenstein, John, *British Artists and the War*, Peter Davies, 1931.

Rothenstein, John, *Modern English Painters*, vol.2, Eyre and Spottiswoode, 1952.

Rothenstein, William, *Men and Memories . . . 1900–1922*, Faber, 1932.

Salis, John, and Montague, C. E., 'Paul Nash', *Country Life*, 1918.

Seddon, Richard, 'Paul Nash 1889–1946', *Studio*, March 1948.

Shand, P. Morton, 'Object and Landscape', *Country Life*, 3 June 1939.

Sieveking, Lance, *The Eye of the Beholder*, Hulton, 1957.

[Tate Gallery] *Modern British Paintings . . . vol.2*, Oldbourne, 1964.

[Tate Gallery] *1972–74 . . . Illustrated Catalogue of Acquisitions*, Tate Gallery, 1975.

Wilenski, R. H., *The Modern Movement in Art*, Faber, 1927.

Wilenski, R. H., 'Carpaccio and Paul Nash', *Studio*, December 1930.

Wilenski, R. H., 'What is the Future of British Painting ?', *World Review*, January 1946.

Wingfield-Digby, George, *Meaning and Symbol in Three Modern Artists*, Faber, 1955.

Lenders

Private Collections

Queen Elizabeth the Queen Mother 203
Anonymous 5, 19, 21, 22, 24, 25, 28, 53, 56, 62, 68,
    69, 72, 79, 83, 87, 92, 93, 94, 95, 96, 98, 104, 110, 114,
    117, 119, 121, 124, 126, 132, 134, 141, 143, 146, 154,
    162, 165, 198, 200, 218, 222, 227, 228, 229, 230, 238
Governor and Company of the Bank of England 152
Dr P. D. Bennett 42
Anthony Bertram 136
Dr E. M. M. Besterman 82
Lord Boyle of Handsworth 66, 168
W. R. Brinton 18
C. L. Brook 155
Mr and Mrs Martin Cardew 13
M. H. Cardiff 186
Mr and Mrs John Carter 89, 176
Castle Howard Collection 54, 59
Lord Clark 173
Mrs Hilda Colinvaux 107
Mr and Mrs William Crabtree 51
Lord Croft 130, 174, 179, 191, 221, 231
Commander Sir Michael Culme-Seymour, Bt. 207, 209
Mrs M. H. Davidson Swift 192
Guy H. Dixon 223
Bernard Donoughue 64
The Viscount Eccles 193
Miss Winifred Felce 73
Mrs Constance J. W. Fettes 105
Mrs Broke Freeman 226
R. D. Girouard 101
The Lord Goodman 30
Executors of the late Adam M. Hamilton 206
A. W. Harris 139
Miss Evelyn Higgins 224
Sir Antony and Lady Hornby 58
Edward James Foundation 116, 123, 129, 140, 156, 157,
    166
Charles Kearley 111
Mrs Audrey Kennett 80, 81
Mrs Enid Levetus 133
George Mitchell 213
Henry Moore 131
Miss Barbara Nash 3, 135
David H. Nash 234
Paul Nash Trustees 238
John Nash 52
Mrs Clare Neilson 108, 170, 188

Anthony d'Offay Gallery 11
Sir Roland Penrose 169
Piccadilly Gallery 61
Benedict Read 9
H. Riley 175
Osborne Robinson 29
Sir John and Lady Rothenstein 8
Royal College of Art, London 217
Norman Satinoff 99
Dr Richard Seddon 236
Richard Smart 167, 194
Victor D. Spark and James Graham and Sons 67
Junior Common Room, St. Annes's College,
    Oxford 142
St. Paul's School, London 153
Mr and Mrs G. R. Strauss 215
Mrs Peter Timms 235
M. A. Vaughan-Lee 199
Vint Trust 112
Estate of W. W. Wadsworth 128
Commander Michael Watson 149
Mrs Oliver Woods 17

Public Collections

Aberdeen Art Gallery 115, 120
Adelaide, Art Gallery of South Australia 122, 125
Belfast, Ulster Museum 100
Birmingham City Museums and Art Gallery 31, 205
Bradford Metropolitan Council, Art Galleries and
    Museums 147
Buffalo, U.S.A., Albright-Knox Art Gallery 150
Cape Town, South African National Gallery 185
Cambridge, Fitzwilliam Museum 14, 196
Cardiff, National Museum of Wales 4
Carlisle Art Gallery 12, 23, 50
Coventry, Herbert Art Gallery 88
Durban Art Gallery, South Africa 177
Edinburgh, Scottish National Gallery of Modern
    Art, 212, 237
Exeter, Royal Albert Memorial Museum and Art
    Gallery 195
Fredericton, New Brunswick, Canada, Beaverbrook
    Art Gallery 158
Glasgow Art Gallery 187
Hamilton Art Gallery, Ontario 178
Harrogate, Borough Art Gallery 103

Hartford, U.S.A., Wadsworth Atheneum   138
Kingston upon Hull, Ferens Art Gallery   204
Leeds City Art Galleries   75, 102, 163, 184
Leicester Museums and Art Galleries   172, 189
Liverpool, Walker Art Gallery   26, 211
London, Arts Council of Great Britain   16, 70
London, Imperial War Museum   38, 39, 40, 41, 44, 46, 47, 48, 190, 208
London, British Council   106, 145, 219
London, British Museum   7, 55, 90, 91
London, Department of the Environment   118, 144
London, Tate Gallery   2, 10, 15, 32, 65, 109, 113, 127, 148, 151, 159, 160, 181, 182, 183
London, Victoria and Albert Museum   1, 6, 20, 27, 34, 161, 233
Manchester, City Art Galleries   33, 36, 85, 86, 171

Manchester, Whitworth Art Gallery   63, 164
Melbourne, National Gallery of Victoria   57, 202, 225
Oldham Art Gallery   232
Ottawa, National Gallery of Canada   35, 37, 45, 49, 76, 84, 220
Paris, Musée National d'Art Moderne   137
Plymouth City Museum and Art Gallery   60
Preston, Harris Museum and Art Gallery   78
Santa Barbara Museum of Art, U.S.A.   214, 216
Sheffield City Art Galleries   180
Southampton Art Gallery   77, 201
Southport, Atkinson Art Gallery   43
Sydney, Art Gallery of New South Wales   97, 197
Toronto, Art Gallery of Ontario   210
Washington, U.S.A., Phillips Collection   74
Wellington, National Art Gallery of New Zealand   71

Photographic Credits

A. C. Cooper
Michael Duffet
J. R. Freeman
Max Machol
Manor, Kay & Foley
John Mills Photography Ltd

Studio Morgan
Helen Muspratt of Ramsey & Muspratt
David Nye
Tom Scott
West Park Studios